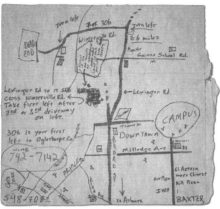

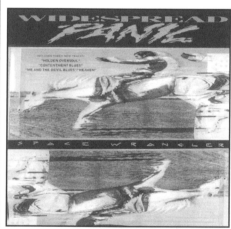

legend of musical symbols

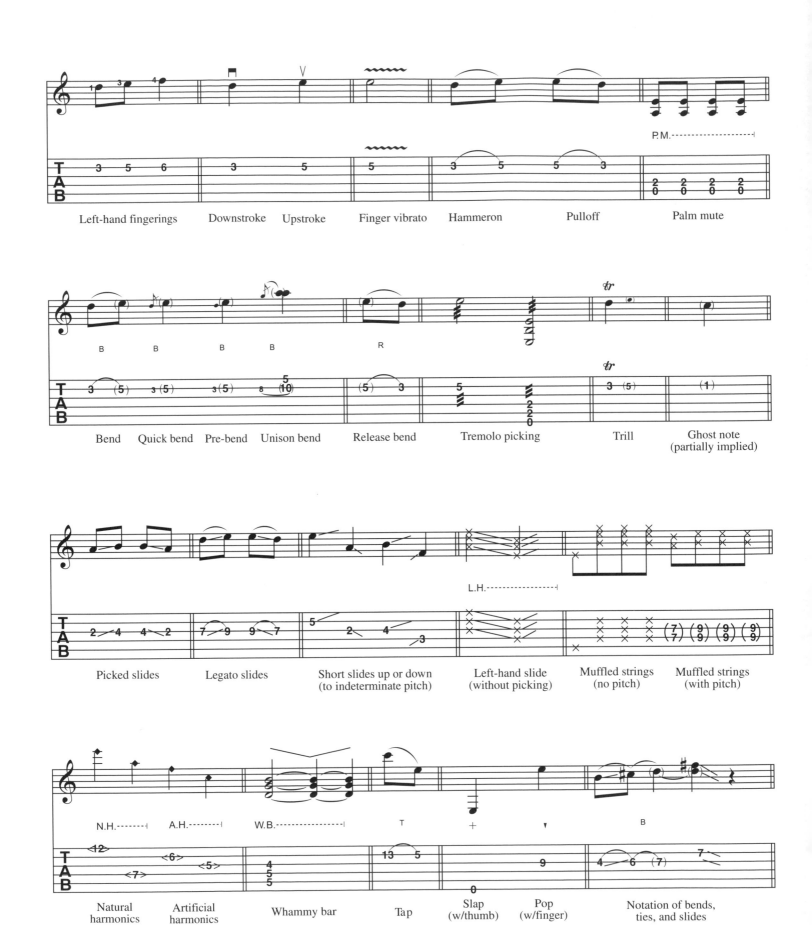

GUITAR TABLATURE EDITION

WIDESPREAD PANIC

SPACE WRANGLER

Amsco Publications
part of the Music Sales Group
New York / Los Angeles /Nashville/ London / Berlin / Copenhagen / Madrid / Paris / Sydney / Tokyo

Front cover art: J. Flournoy Holmes / Art & Death
Cover design: Sarah Nesenjuk
Project editor: David Bradley
Transcriptions: Hemme Luttjeboer

This book © 2006 by Amsco Publications,
A Division of Music Sales Corporation, New York

Order No. AM 981860
ISBN: 0.8256.3341.9

Exclusive Distributors:
Music Sales Corporation
257 Park Avenue South, New York, NY 10010 USA
Music Sales Limited
14-15 Berners Street, London W1T 3LJ England
Music Sales Pty. Limited
120 Rothschild Street, Rosebery, Sydney, NSW 2018, Australia

Printed in the United States of America by
Vicks Lithograph and Printing Corporation

table of contents

chilly water

By John F. Bell, Michael N. Houser, Todd A. Nance and David Schools

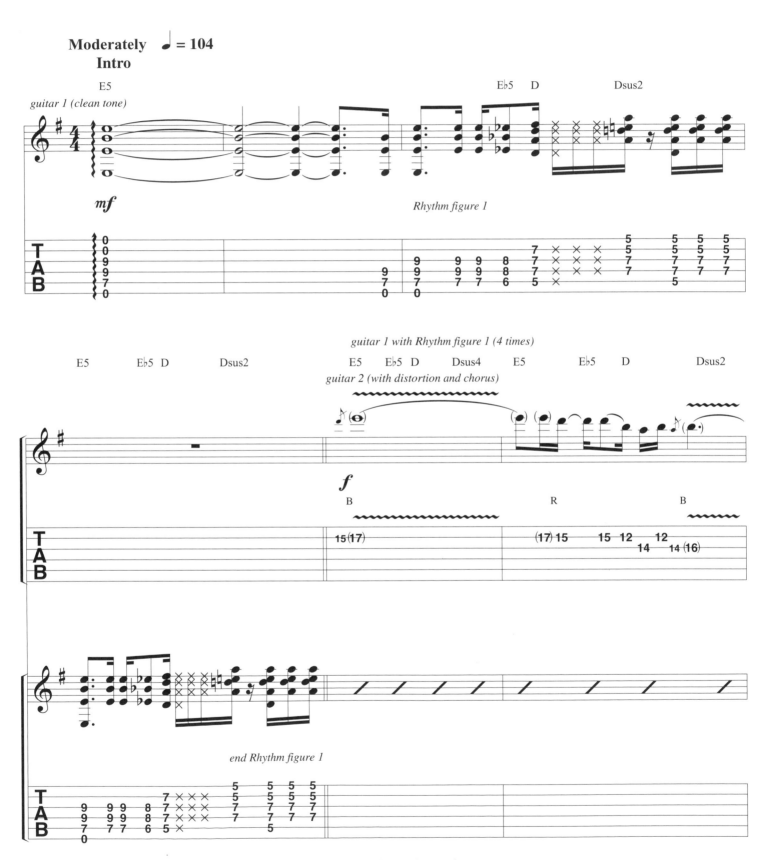

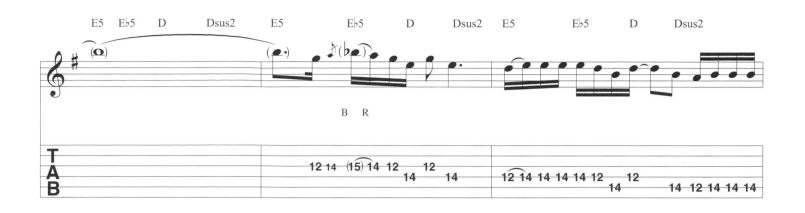

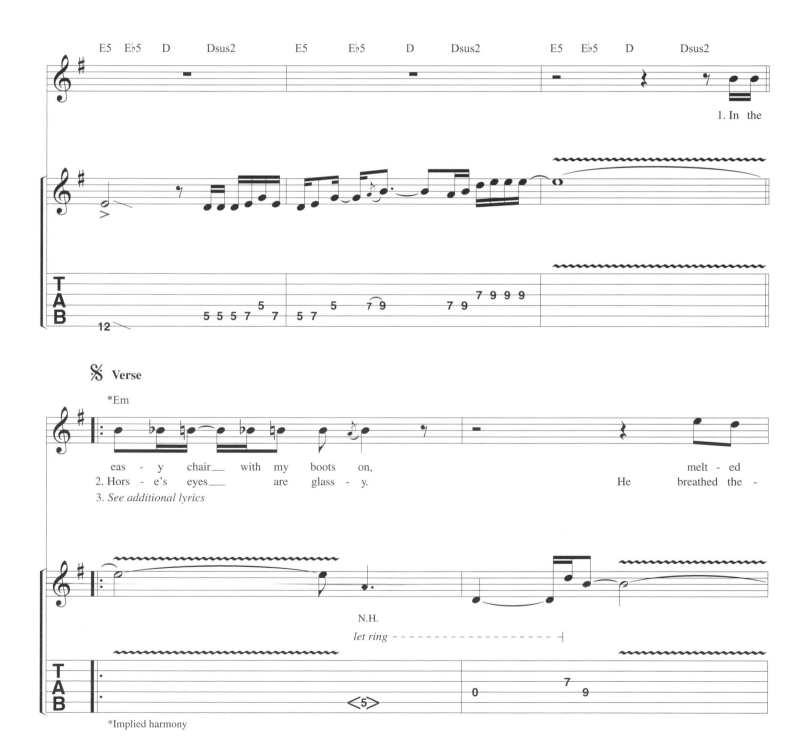

whis - key in___ my hand.___
cit - y in his lungs last night.

I
I

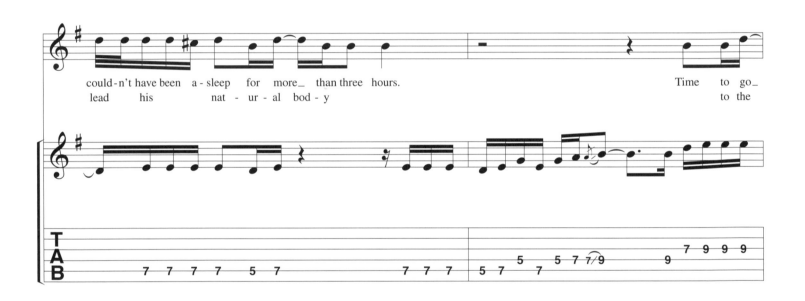

could-n't have been a - sleep for more___ than three hours.
lead his nat - ur - al bod - y

Time to go___
to the

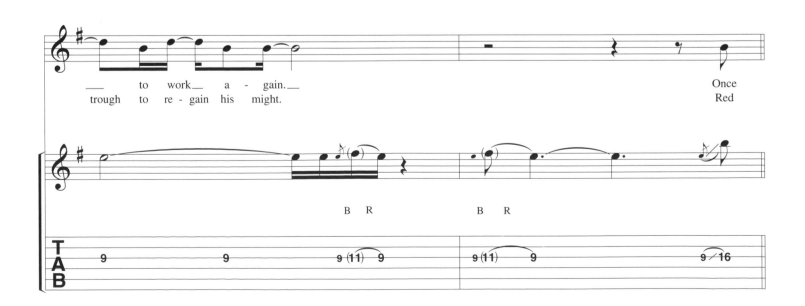

___ to work___ a - gain.___
trough to re - gain his might.

Once
Red

Pre-chorus

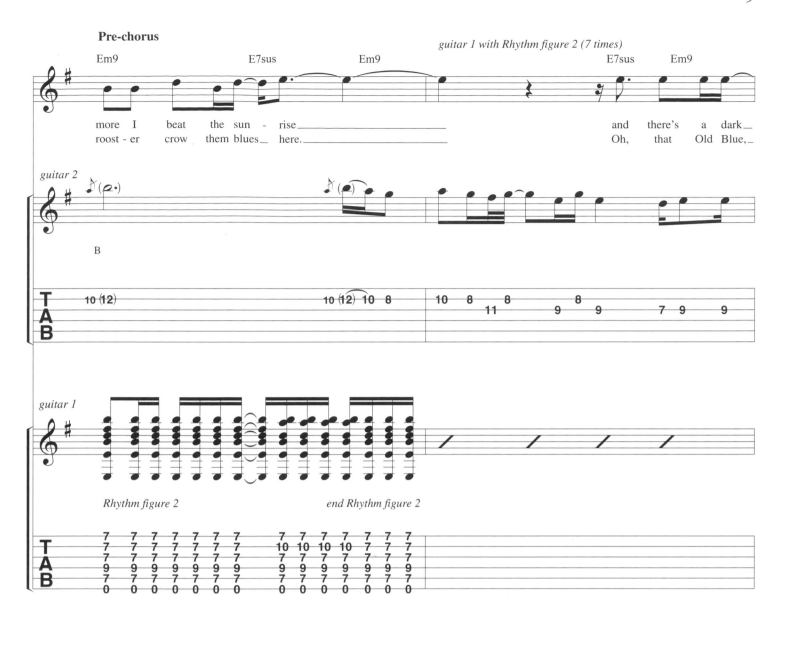

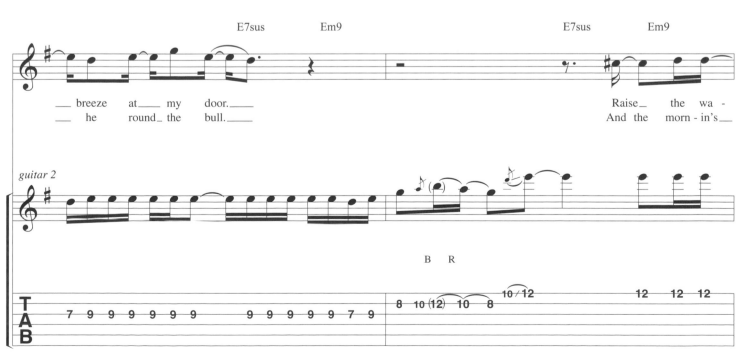

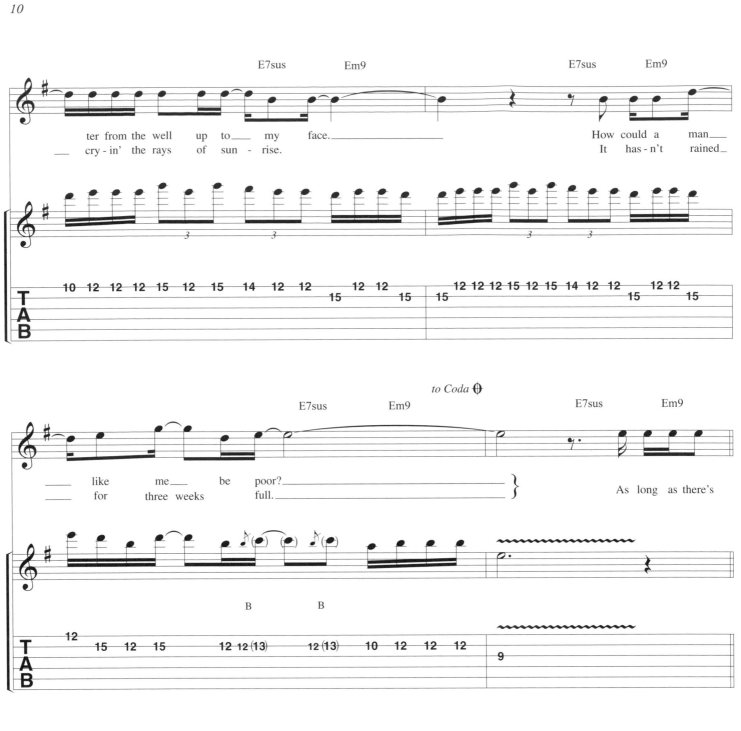

ter from the well   up to___ my   face._____
___ cry - in' the rays   of   sun - rise.

How could a   man___
It   has - n't   rained___

to Coda ⊕

___ like   me___ be   poor?_____
___ for   three weeks   full._____

As long as there's

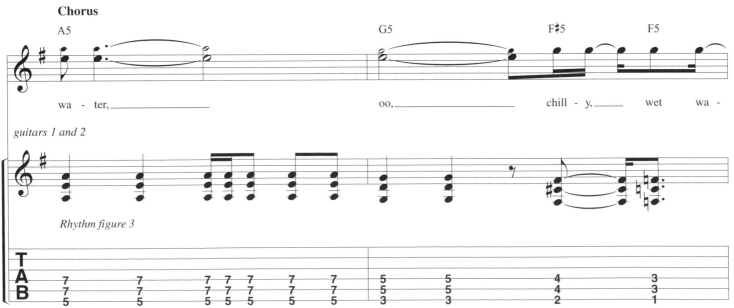

Chorus

guitars 1 and 2

wa - ter,_____   oo,_____ chill - y,_____ wet wa -

Rhythm figure 3

end Rhythm figure 3

guitars 1 and 2 with Rhythm figure 3

Oo, gim - me some__ of that_____ cool wa - ter.

1.
*Em
guitar 2

B R

*Implied harmony

2. Well, my

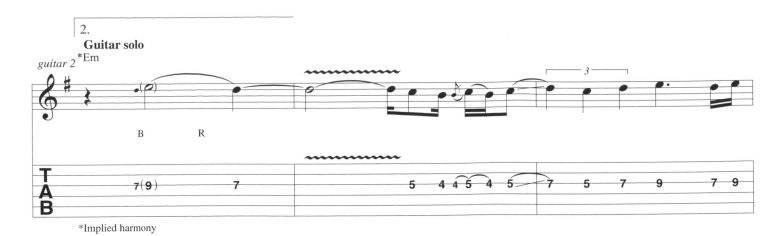

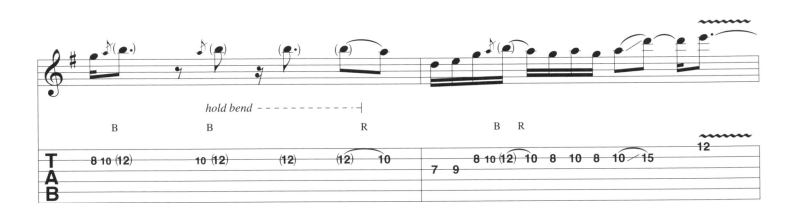

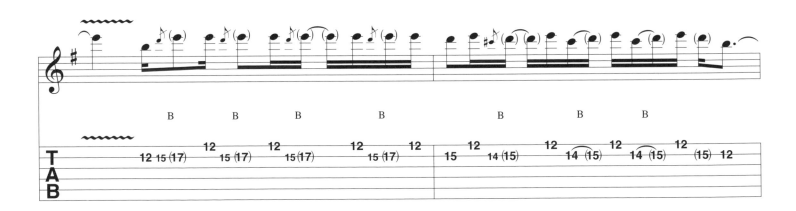

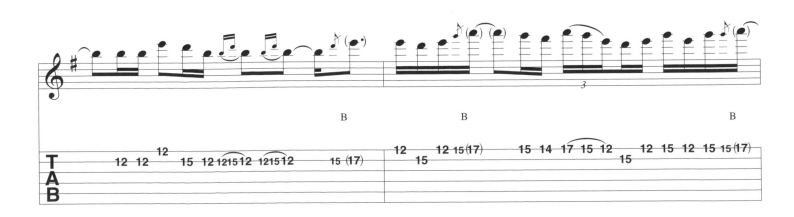

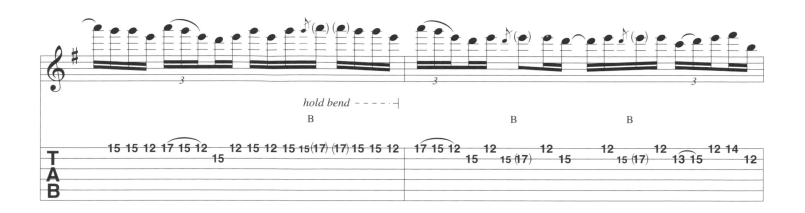

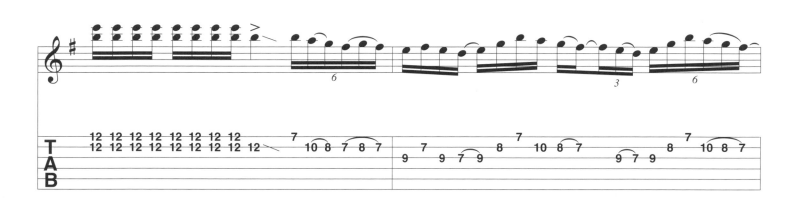

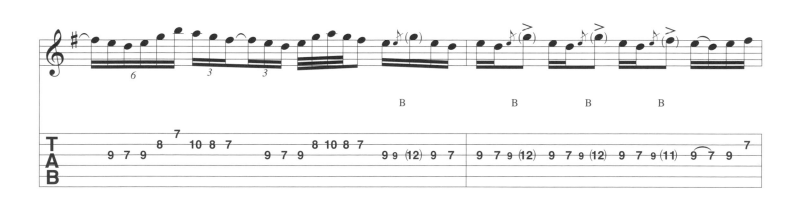

*guitar 1 with Rhythm figure 3 (2 times)

A5

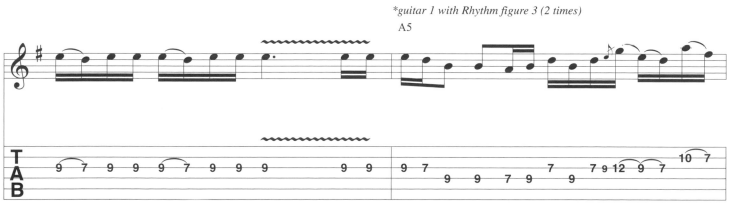

*keyboards arranged for guitar

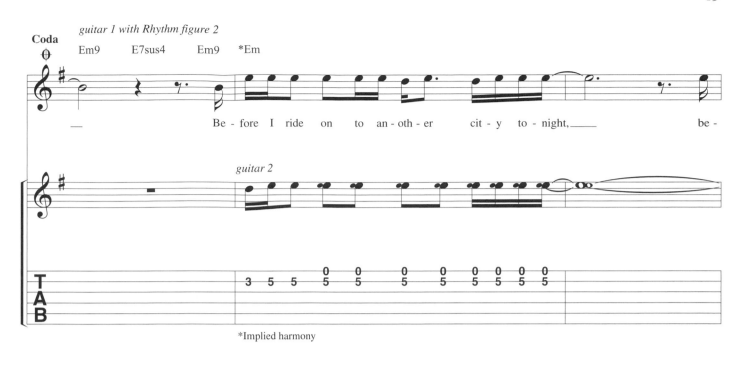

*Implied harmony

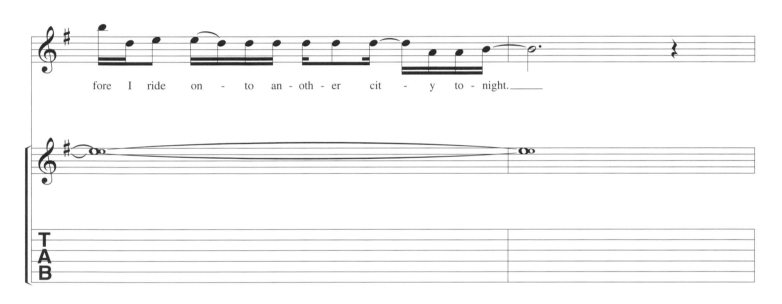

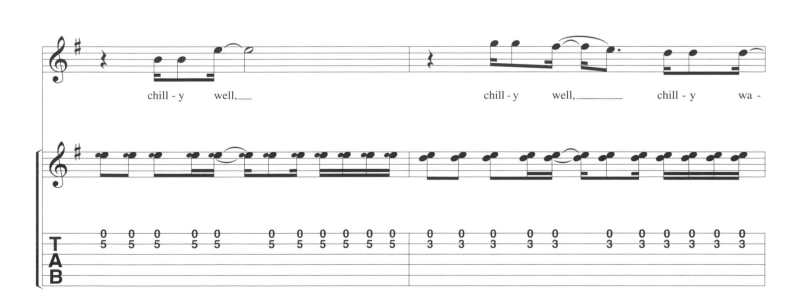

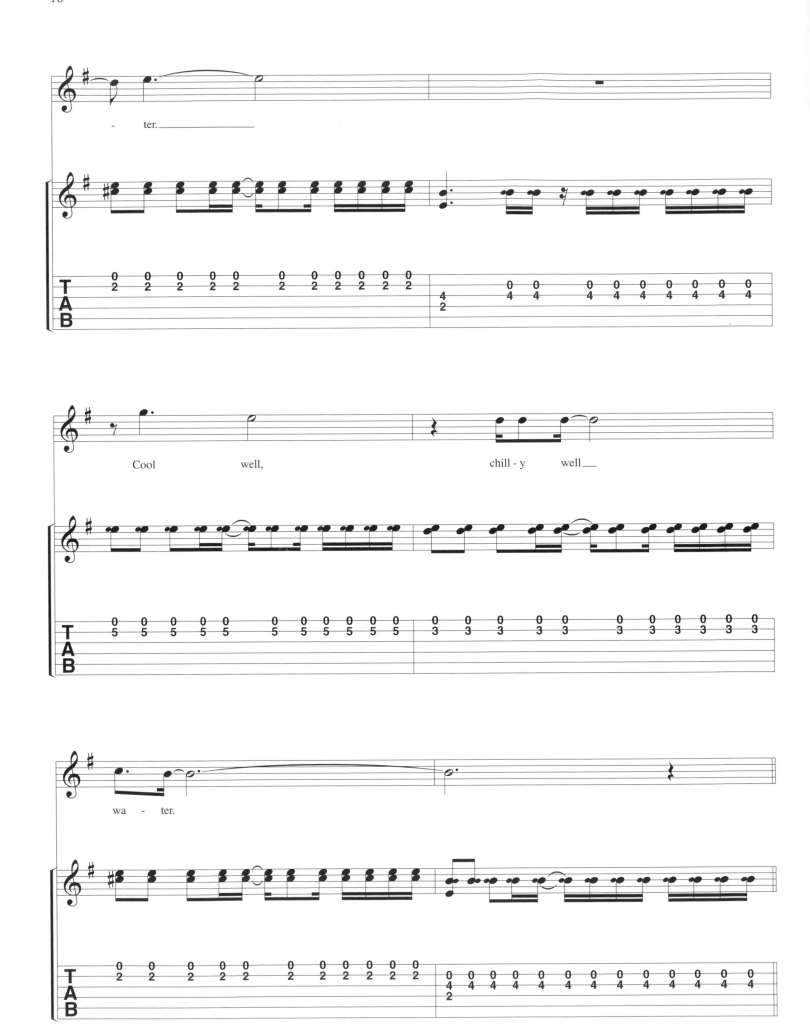

Outro

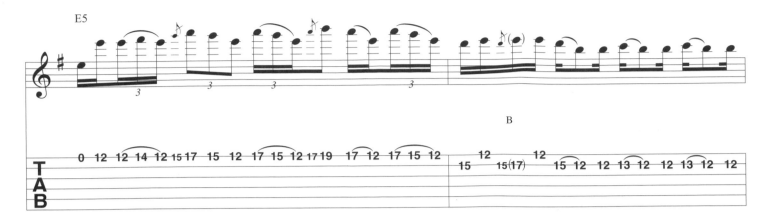

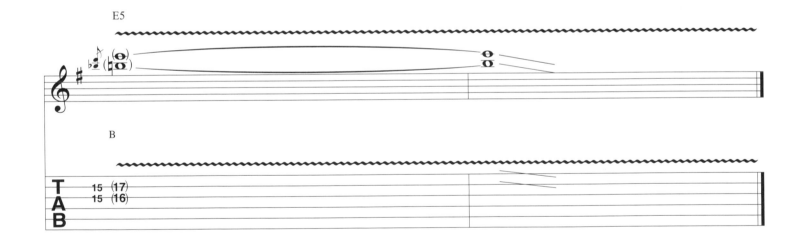

Verse
3. Venus light is rising.
   I lay my buckets inside the shed.
   And there's a man I see – a stranger,
   Leaning on the gate outside my fence.

Pre-Chorus
Said, "I'm riding out from the city
Where they started holding water back last night.
I was hoping I could get a drink from your well
Before I ride on to another city tonight."

travelin' light

By J.J. Cale

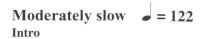

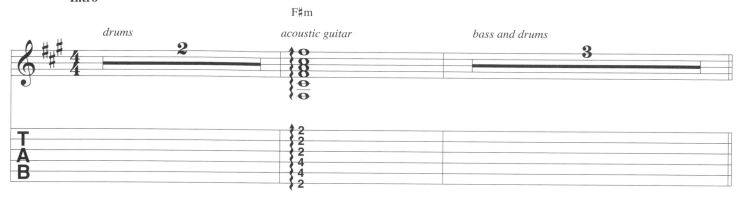

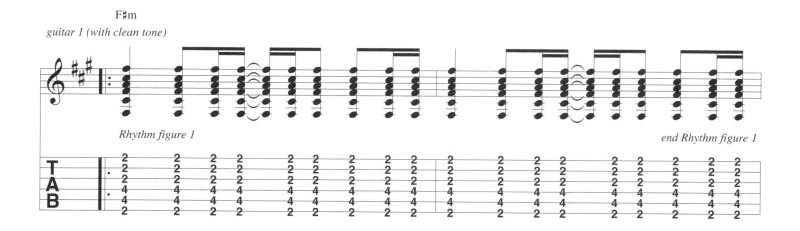

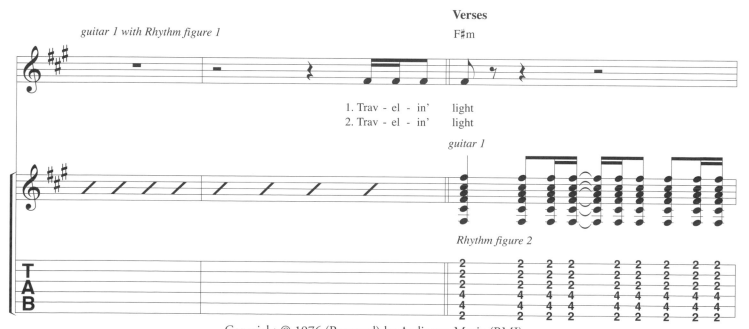

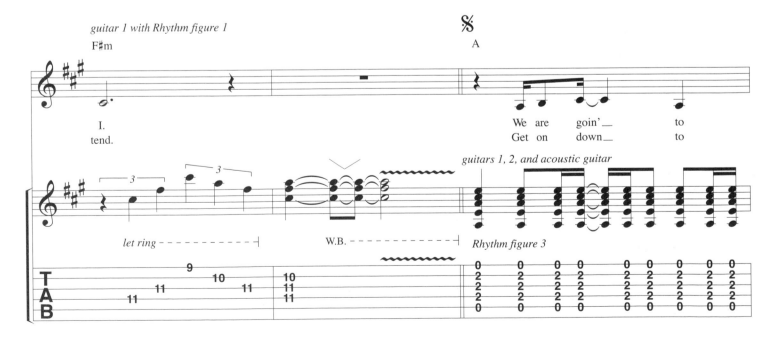

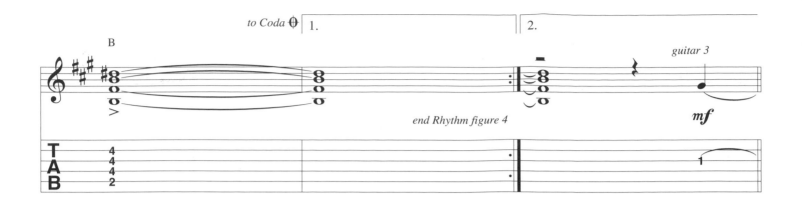

Guitar solo
guitars 1, 2, and acoustic guitar with Rhythm figure 1 (2 times)

guitars 1, 2, and acoustic guitar with Rhythm figure 2

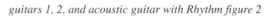

guitars 1, 2, and acoustic guitar with Rhythm figure 2

guitars 1, 2, and acoustic guitar with Rhythm figure 1

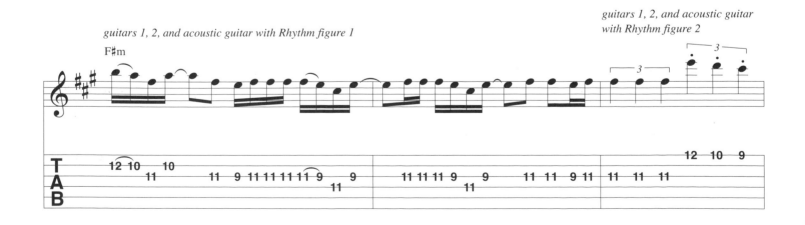

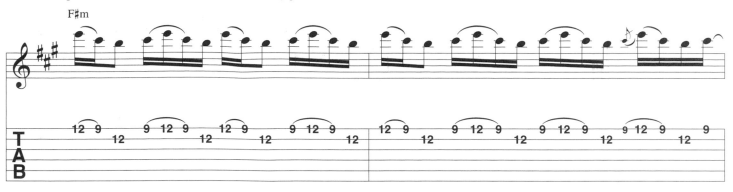

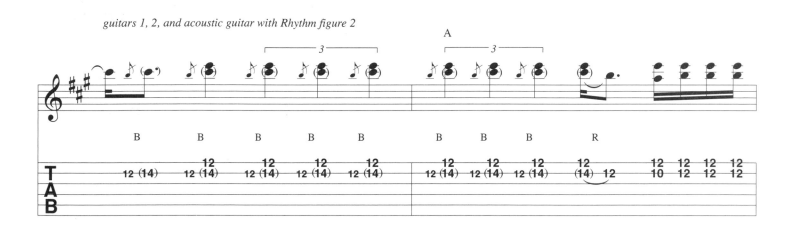

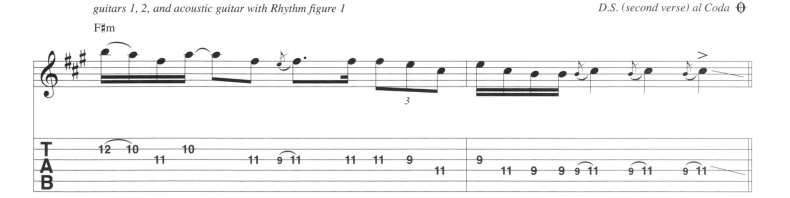

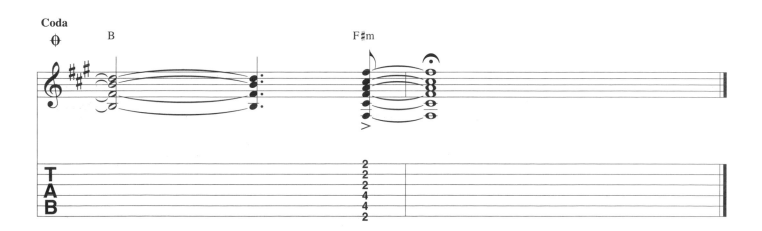

space wrangler

By John F. Bell, Michael N. Houser, Todd A. Nance and David Schools

Moderately fast ♩ = 134

Intro

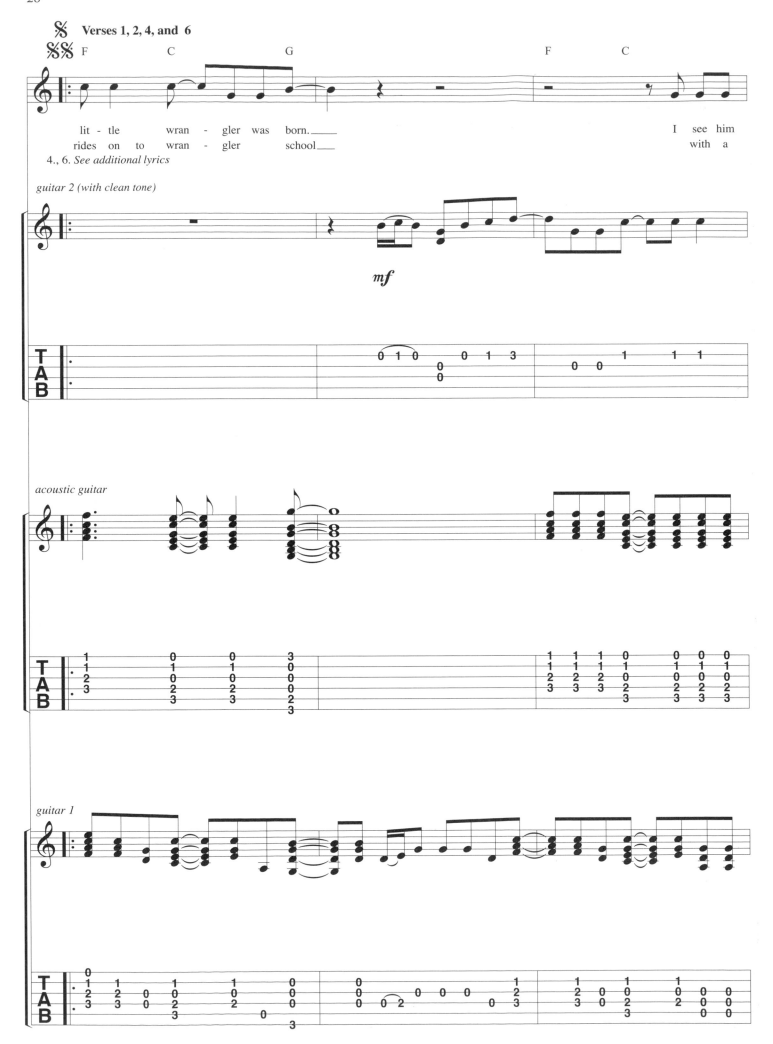

𝄋 **Verses 1, 2, 4, and 6**

lit - tle wran - gler was born._____ I see him
rides on to wran - gler school_____ with a

4., 6. See additional lyrics

guitar 2 (with clean tone)

acoustic guitar

guitar 1

squirm - ing   in   the   sad - dle   all   wet   and   warm.
sling - shot   and   a   sad - dle bag   of   hand - me - down tools.

He's
He

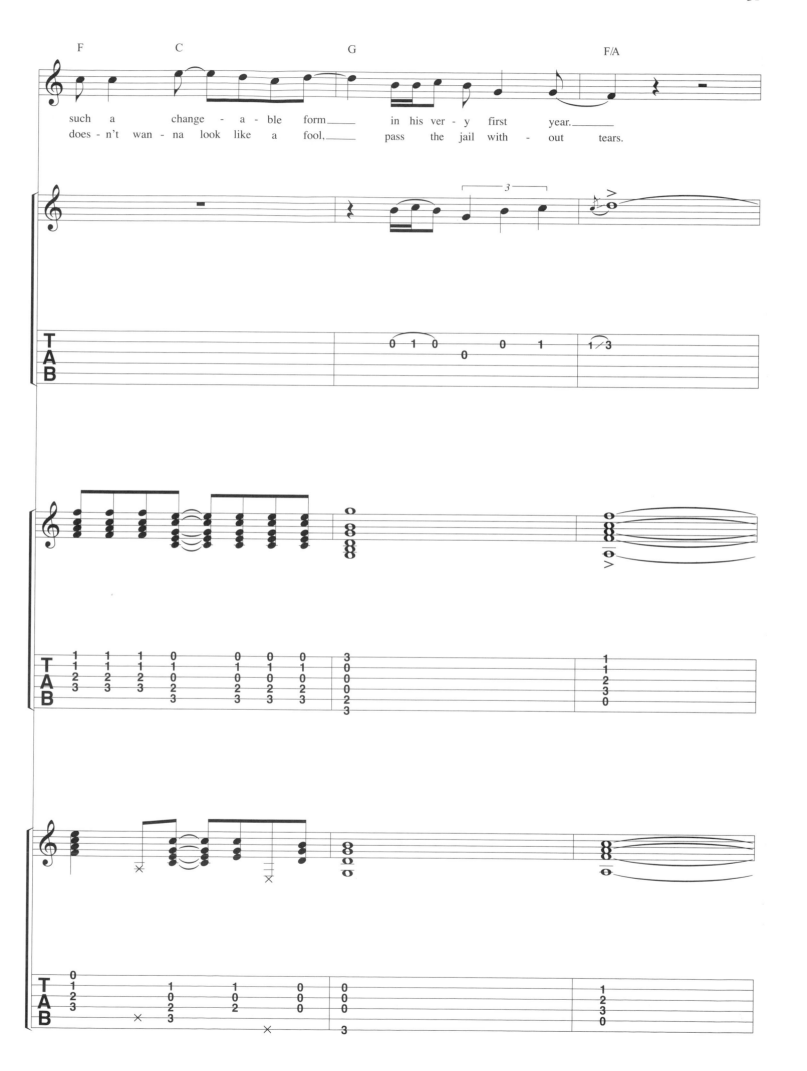

such a   change - a - ble form_____   in his ver - y first   year._____
does - n't   wan - na   look like a   fool,_____   pass the jail with - out   tears.

Interlude

Verses 3 and 5

3. Time ma - chines_____ re - mem - bered scenes that a
5. Time ma - chines_____ new rou - tines that a

wran - gler rides____ through a pass - ing stream. Oh,____
wran - gler rides____ through a pass - ing dream. Oh,____

time's re - placed_____ by a peace - ful dream._____
time's re - placed_____ by a peace - ful stream._____

guitar 2

D.S. al second ending
D.S.S. al Coda ⊕

4. He   reigns   his
6. He   gets   off

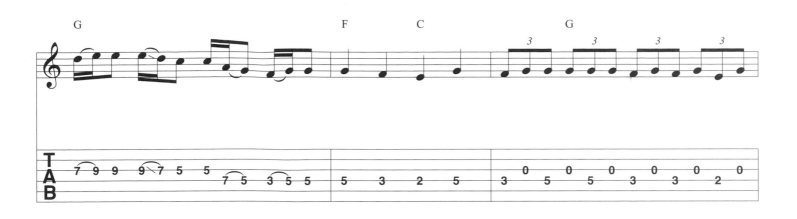

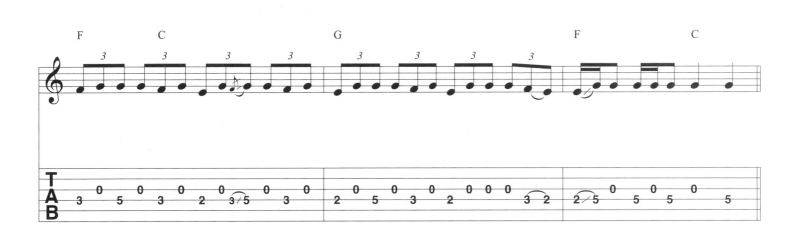

Outro

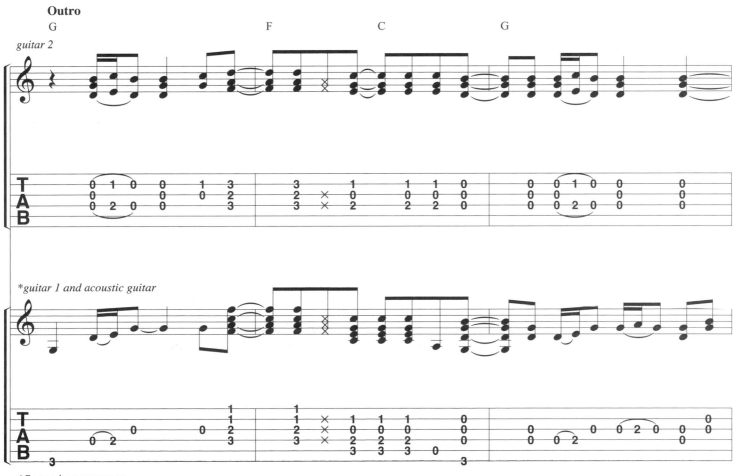

Composite arrangement

Verse

4. He reigns his pony to the gate of the school.
   Feather pens and inkwells of hand-me-down rules.
   Like trading a pony for an aging mule,
   He rides away without fear.

6. He gets off at a stranger's place
   Where the girls dance different with familiar grace.
   He's knowing that he found the place
   That pours cold, cold beer.

coconut

By John F. Bell, Michael N. Houser, Todd A. Nance and David Schools

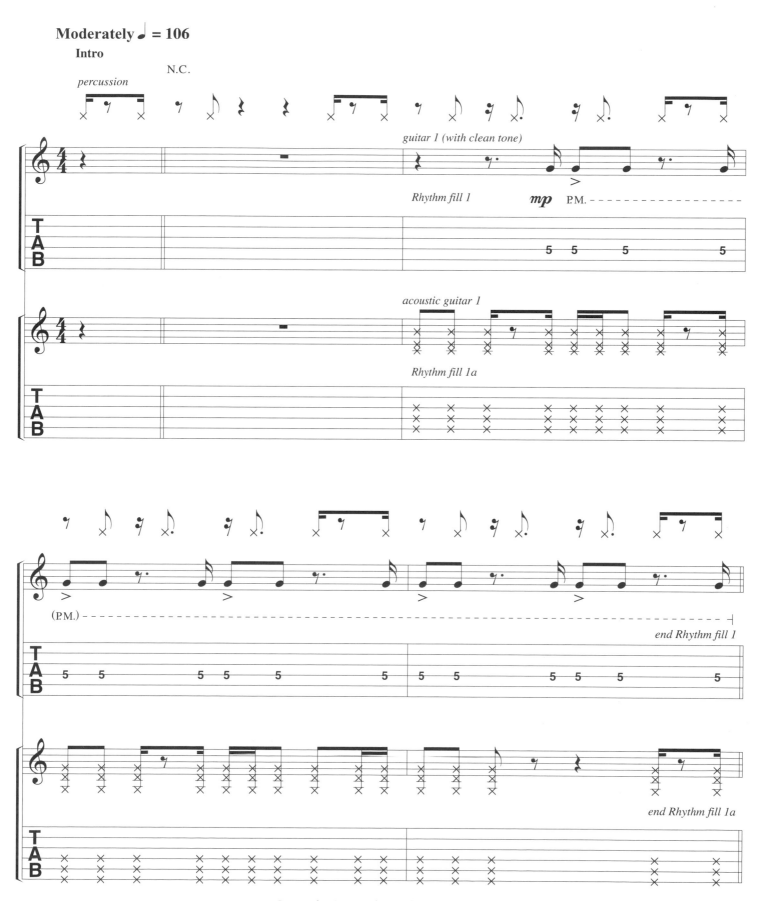

Chorus

guitar 1 and acoustic guitar 1 with Rhythm fills 1 and 1a
percussion simile

I_____ like co - co - nuts. You can break them o - pen, they smell like lad - ies

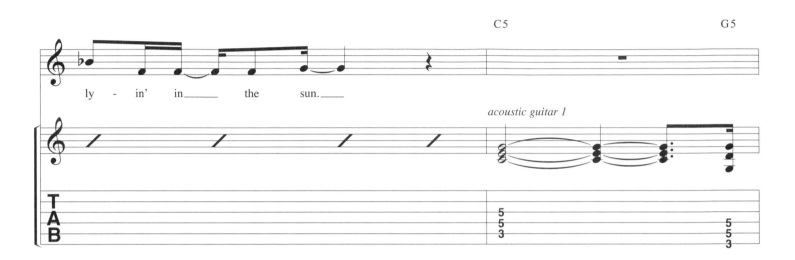

C5   G5

ly - in' in_____ the sun._____

acoustic guitar 1

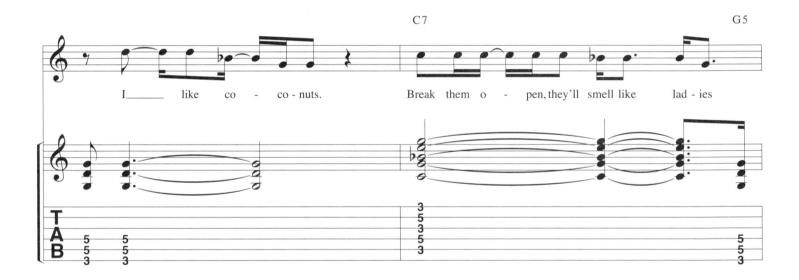

C7   G5

I_____ like co - co - nuts. Break them o - pen, they'll smell like lad - ies

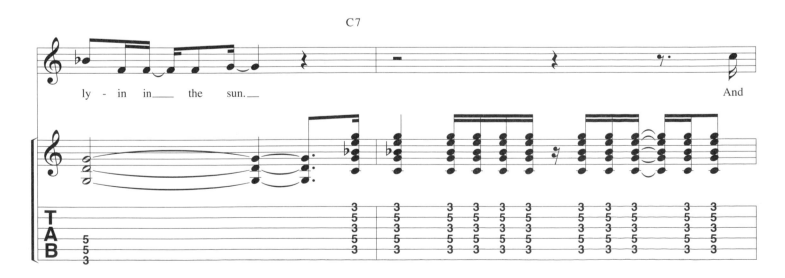

C7

ly - in in_____ the sun._____   And

if I had___ my way___   I'd give a co - co - nut to ev - 'ry - one.___

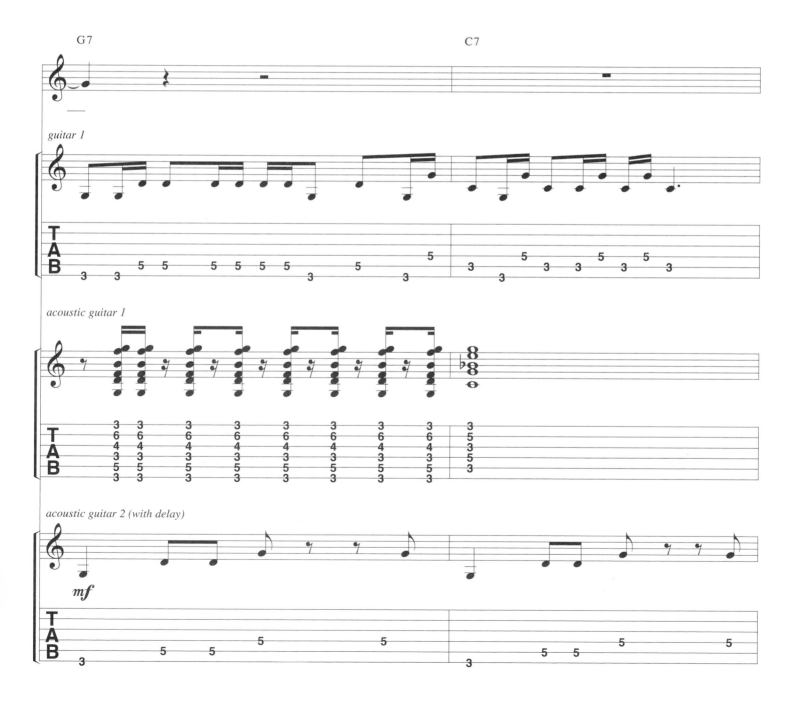

Interlude

Verse

1. I got a friend_ named Jack,

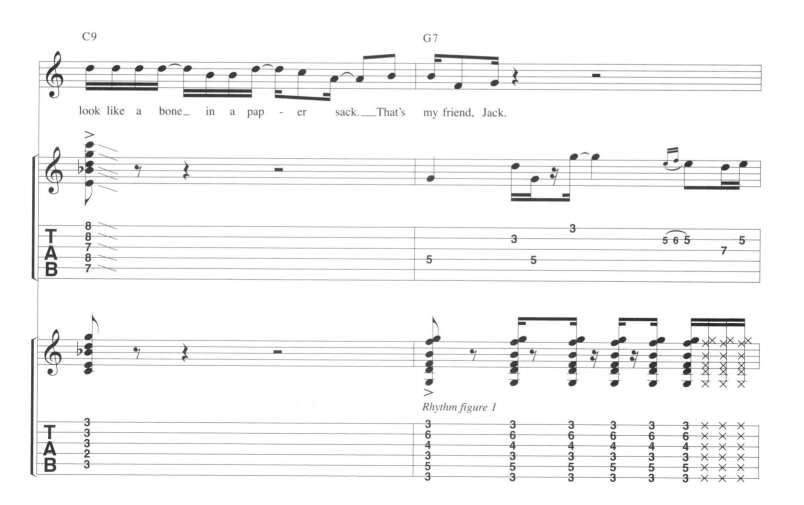

look like a bone_ in a pap - er sack. ___ That's my friend, Jack.

Rhythm figure 1

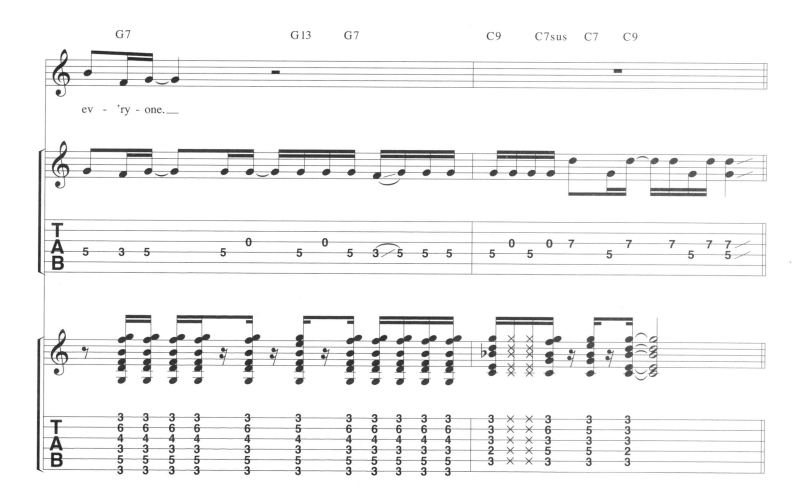

Verse
acoustic guitar 1 with Rhythm figure 1 (4 times)

2. Jack - ie likes the smell_ of cut grass. He used to play ball on Sat - ur - days,_

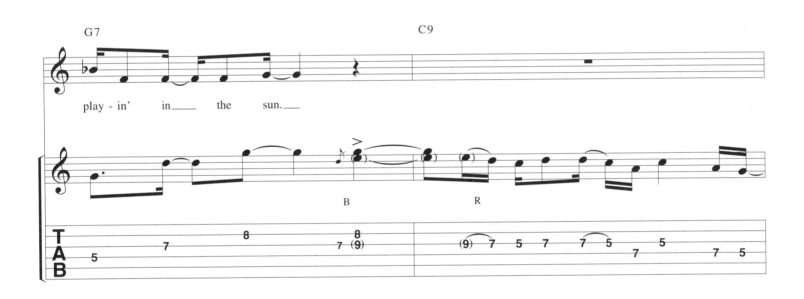

play - in' in_ the sun._

Jack - ie likes the smell_ of cut grass. He used to play ball on Sat - ur - days,_

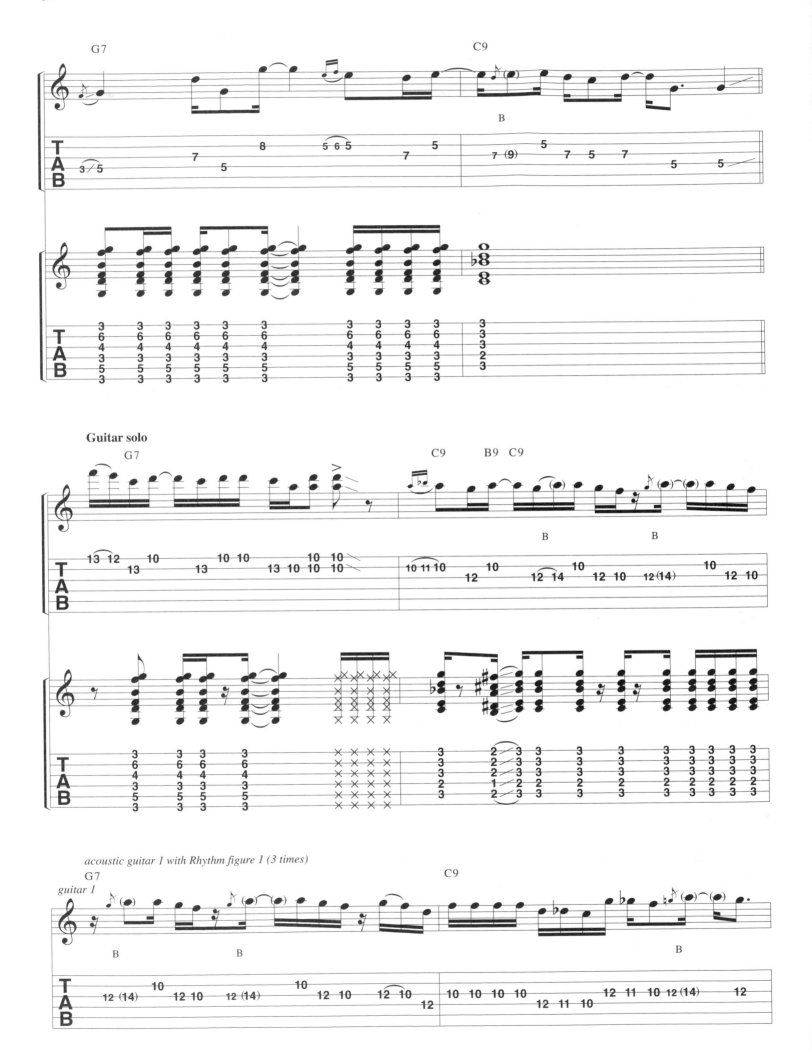

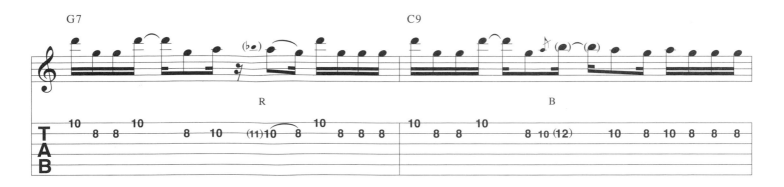

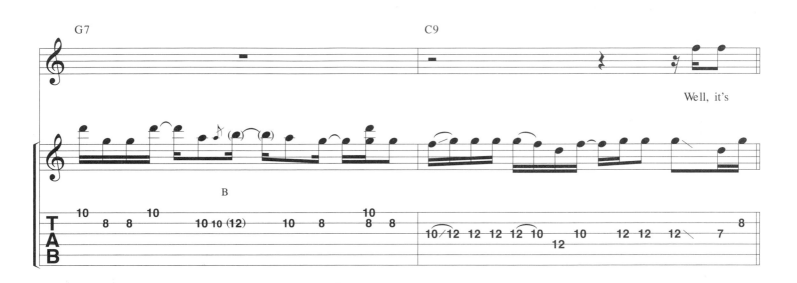

Well, it's

Bridge

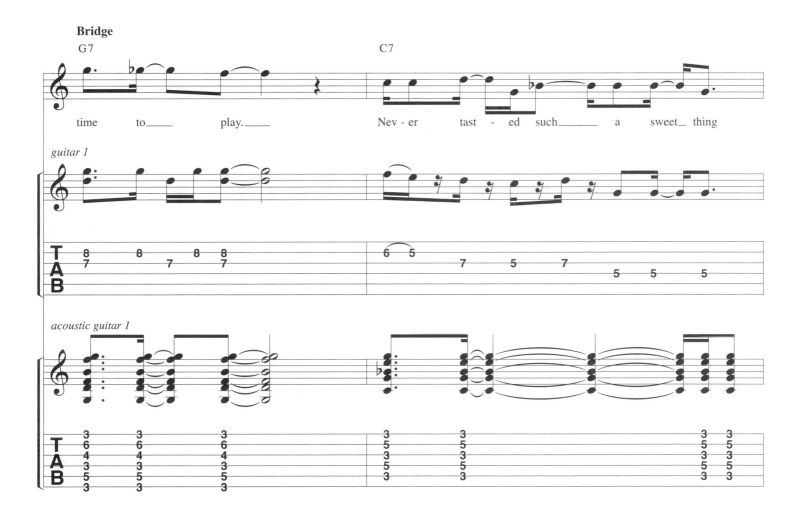

time to____ play.____ Nev - er tast - ed such____ a sweet__ thing

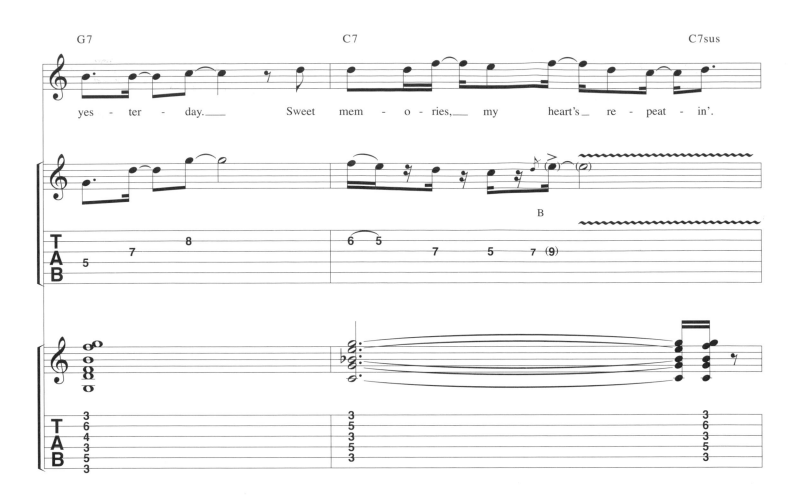

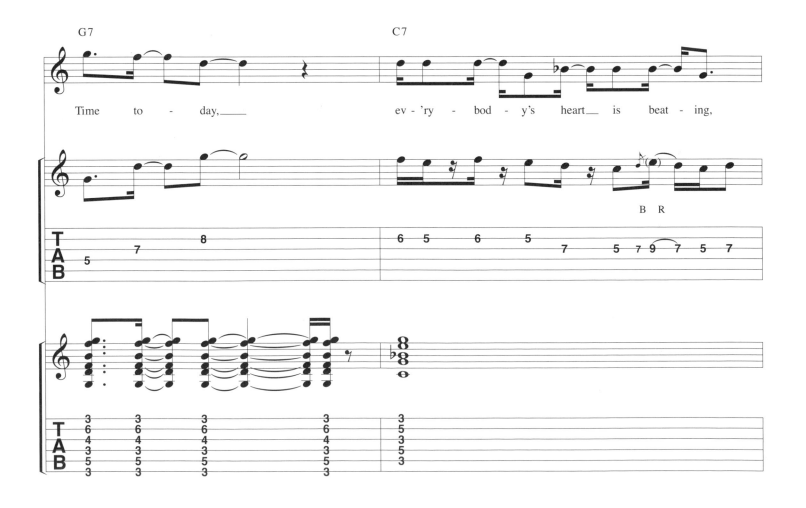

ev - 'ry - bod - y's smile_ is greet - in', ev - 'ry - bod - y's soul_ is heat - in'.

Interlude

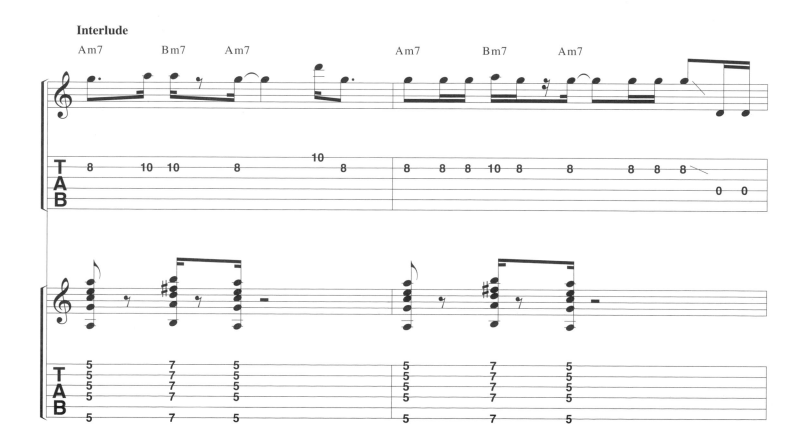

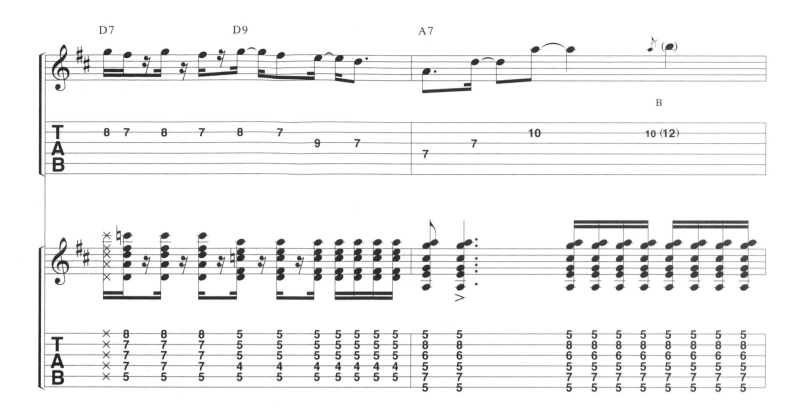

Verse

3. Well, I know a guy____ named Fred.

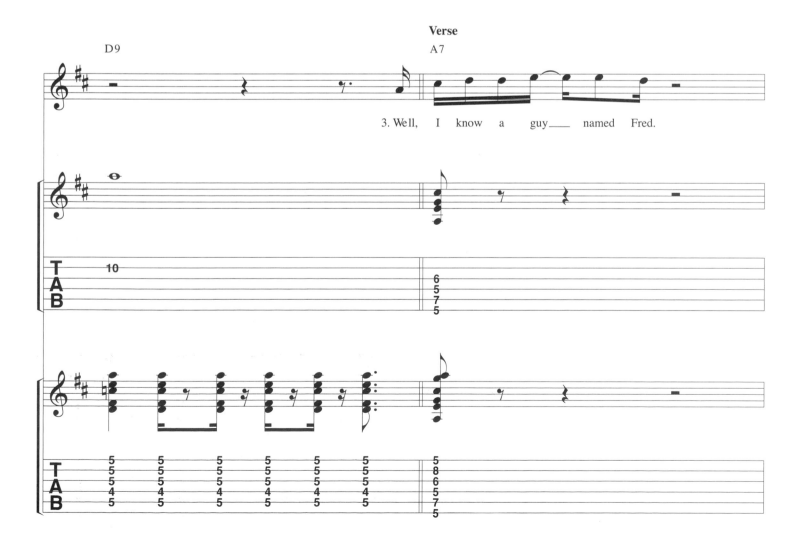

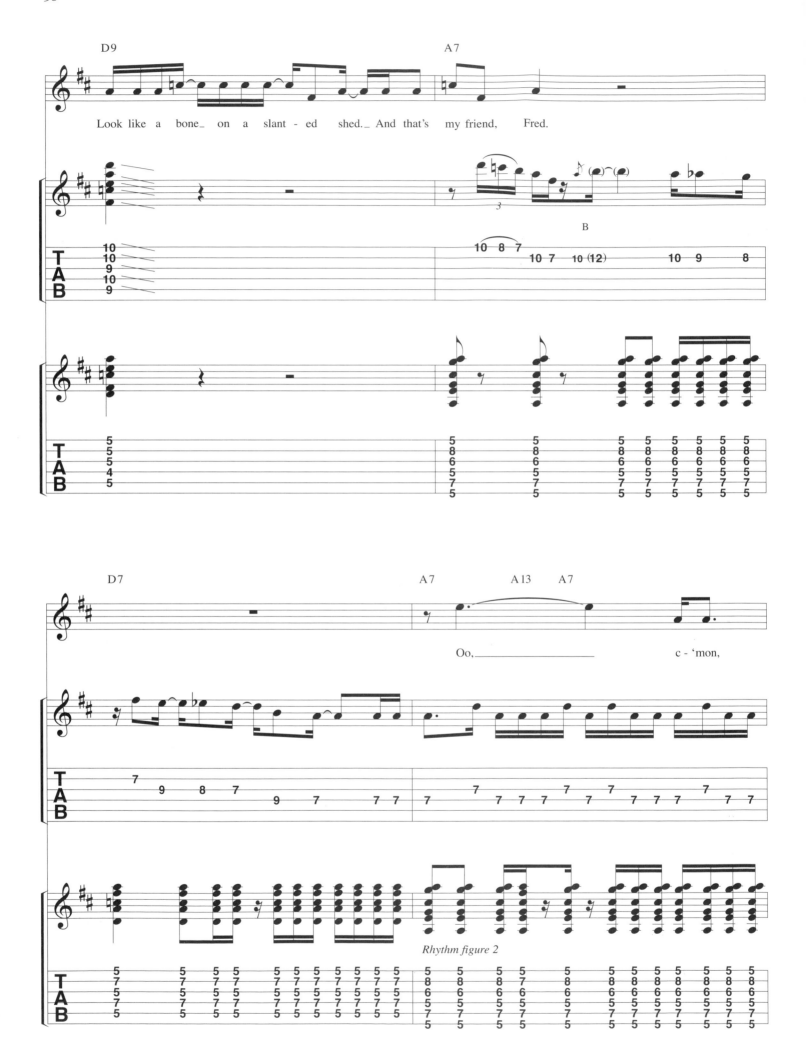

Look like a bone_ on a slant-ed shed._ And that's my friend, Fred.

Oo,_____ c-'mon,

Rhythm figure 2

acoustic guitar 1 with Rhythm figure 2 (7 times)

Fred, smell these co - co - nuts.

end Rhythm figure 2

There's e - nough for ev - 'ry - one.__

guitar 1

Oo, ev - 'ry - one.__

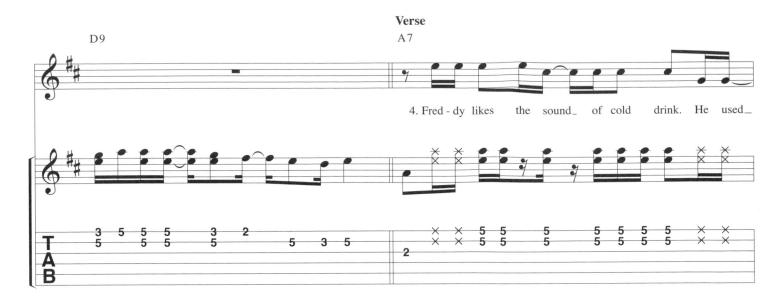

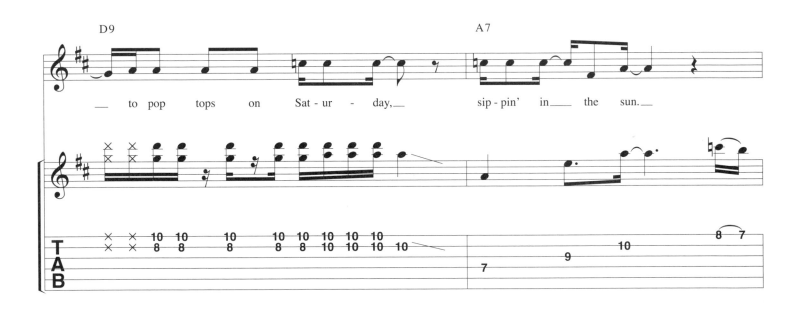

to pop tops on Sat - ur - days.__ He was sip - pin' in__ the sun.__

If Fred - dy had__ his way__

Guitar solo

he'd give a cold drink to ev - 'ry - one.

Rhythm figure 3

acoustic guitar 1 with Rhythm figure 3 (7 times)

end Rhythm figure 3

Outro

acoustic guitar 1 with Rhythm figure 3 (2 times)

Background vocal: I'm gon - na   *(second time:)* I_____ like

fol - low my nose_ to where the co - co - nut   grows.

No - bod - y knows_ like my_ nose.

lad - ies ly - in' in_ the sun._

My nose knows._____

1. - 3.

4.

I'm gon - na

the take out

By John F. Bell, Michael N. Houser, Todd A. Nance and David Schools

*violin arranged for guitar

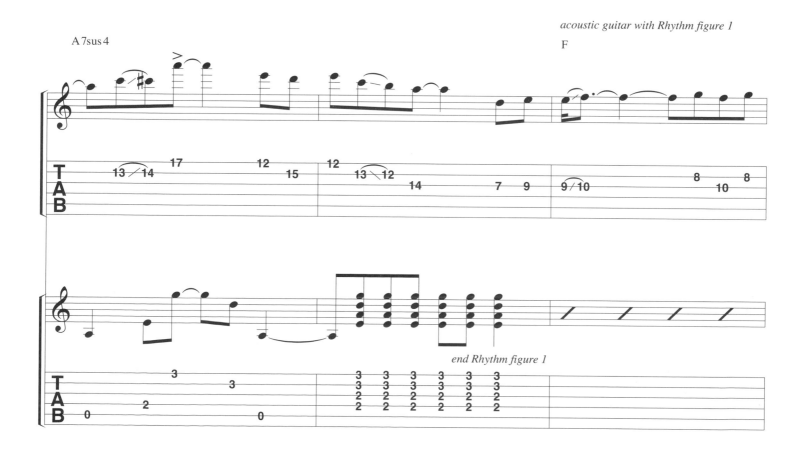

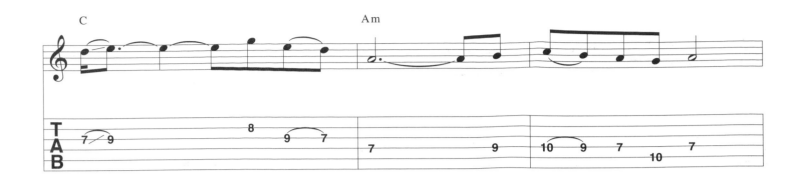

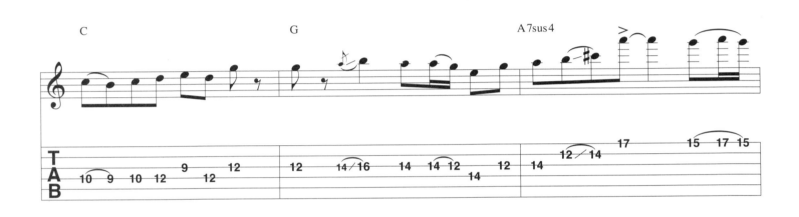

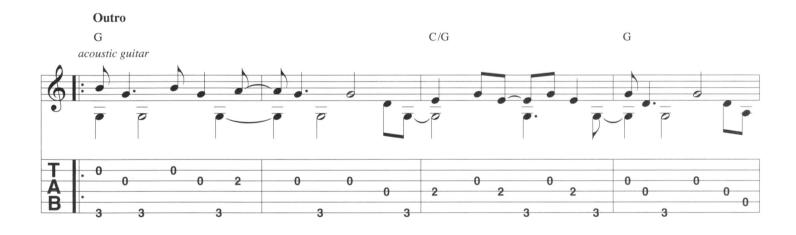

Outro

acoustic guitar

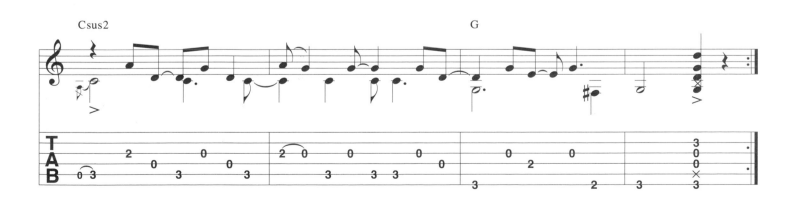

porch song

By John F. Bell, Michael N. Houser, Todd A. Nance and David Schools

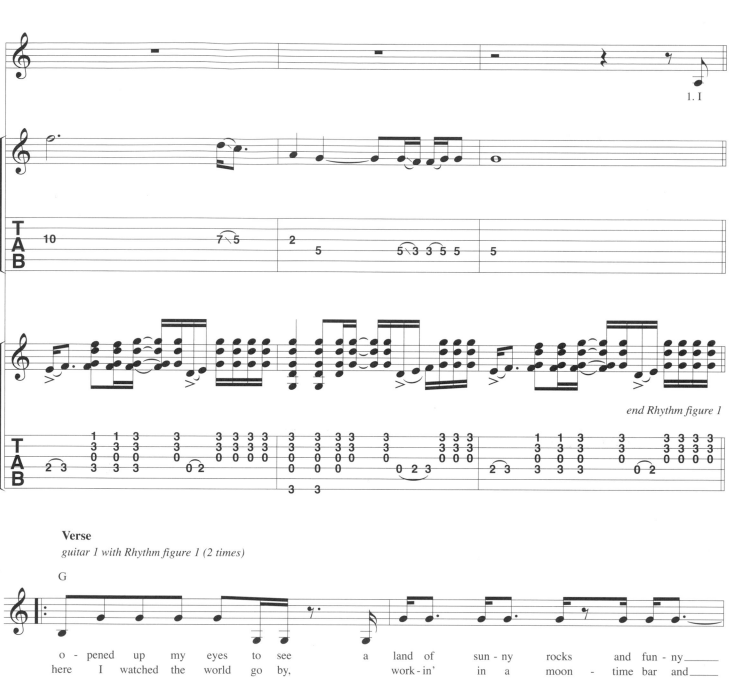

end Rhythm figure 1

Verse

guitar 1 with Rhythm figure 1 (2 times)

o - pened up my eyes to see a land of sun - ny rocks and fun - ny_____

here I watched the world go by, work - in' in a moon - time bar and_____

___ trees._____

___ grill._____

Guess I'm on the moon___ a - gain, a

The word from Earth; my time is up, but

heav - y earth ex - change, a light - er_____ breeze.

here up - on the moon the time stands_____ still.

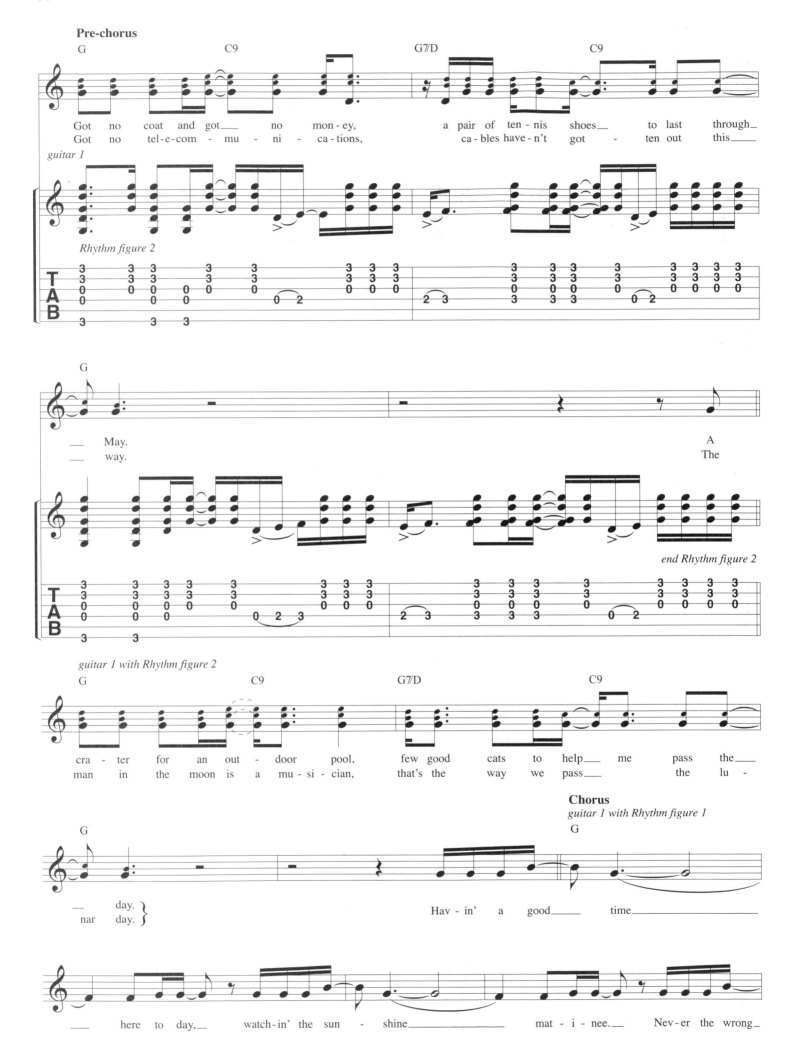

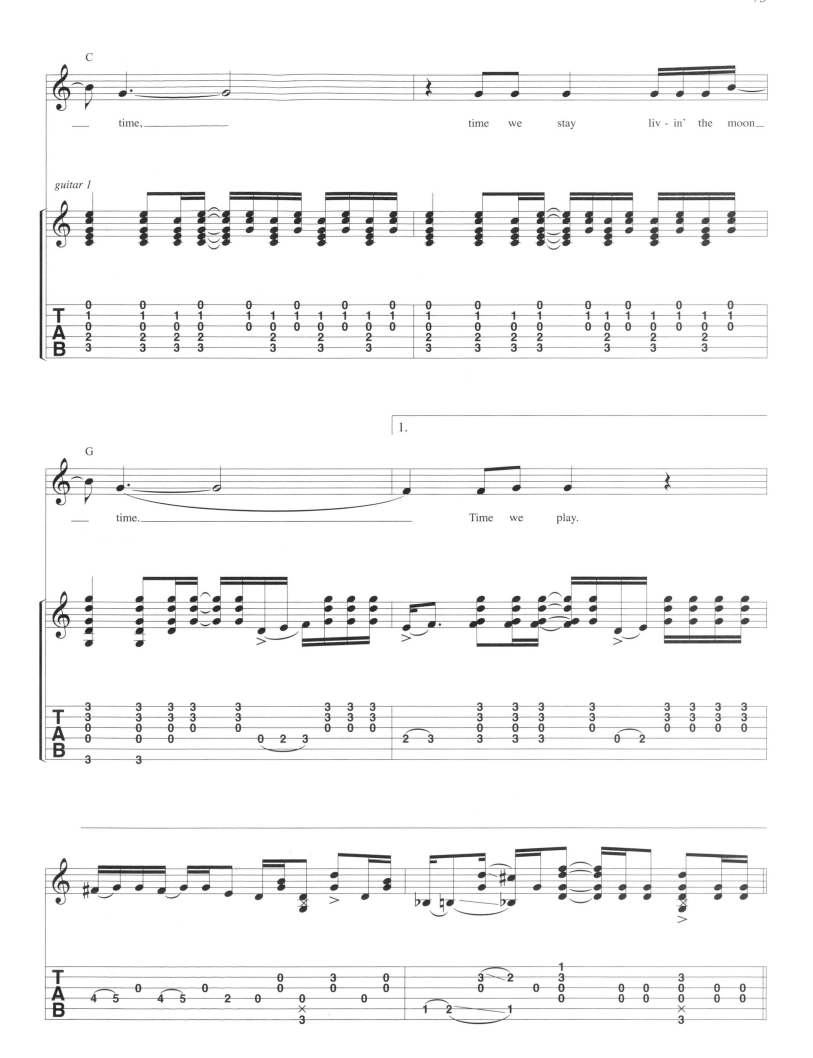

Interlude
guitar 1 with Rhythm figure 1

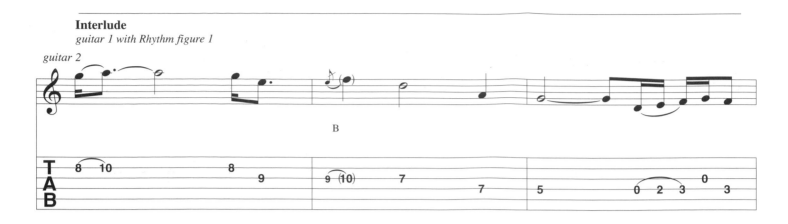

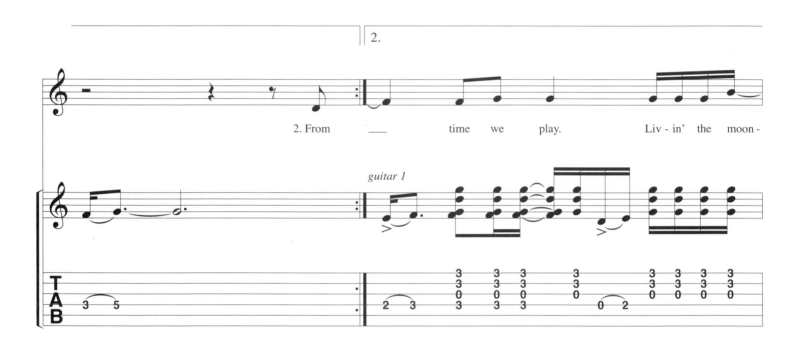

2. From ___ time we play. Liv - in' the moon-

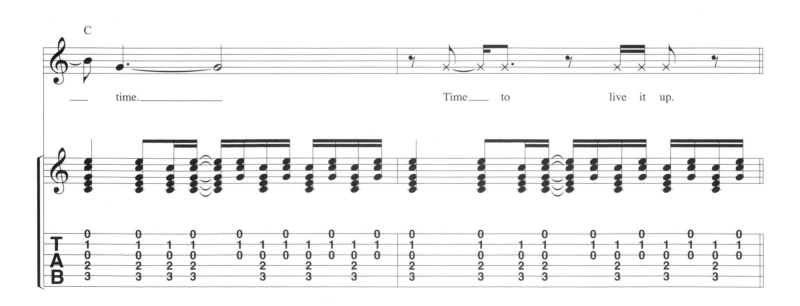

___ time. _____ Time ___ to live it up.

Outro

stop-go

By John F. Bell, Michael N. Houser, Todd A. Nance and David Schools

Moderately ♩ = 104

Intro

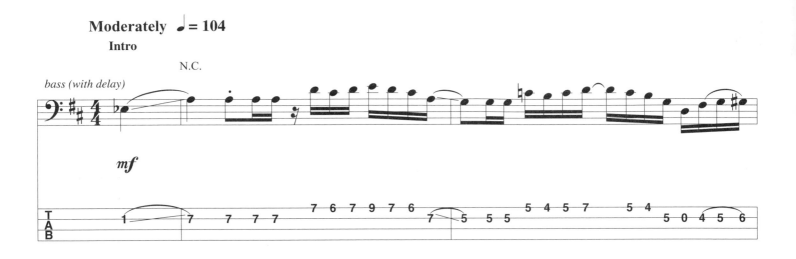

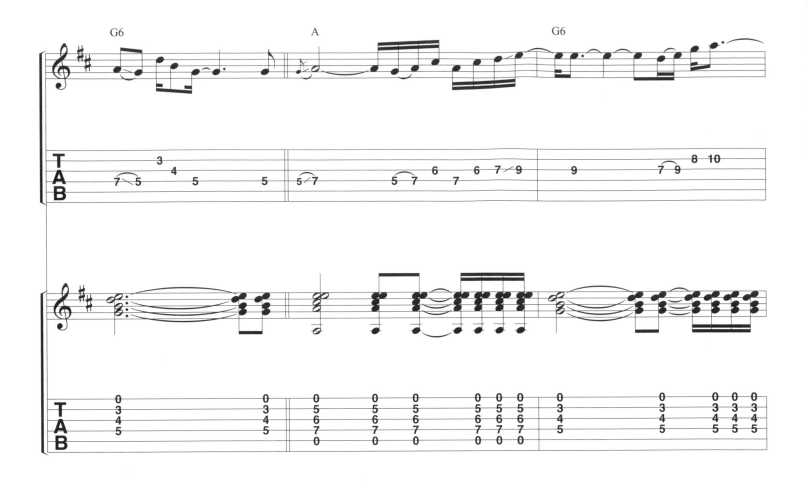

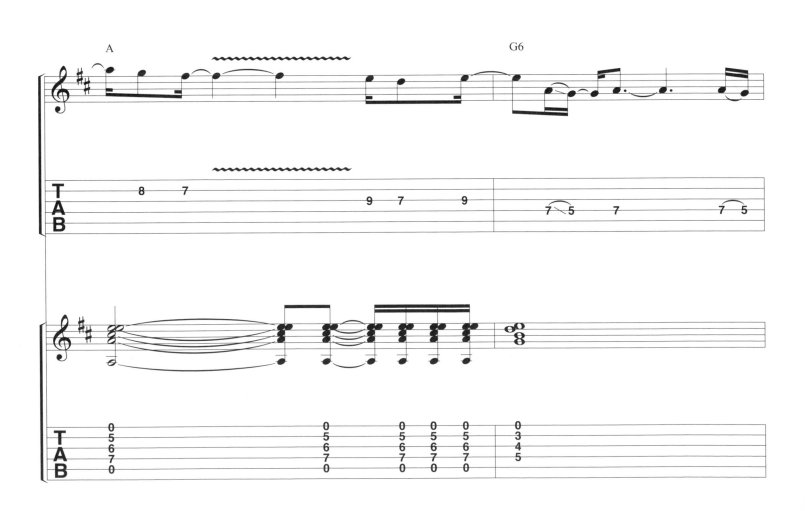

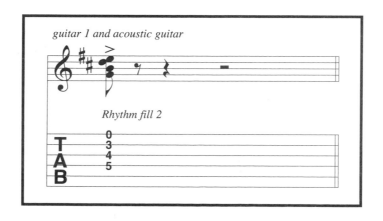

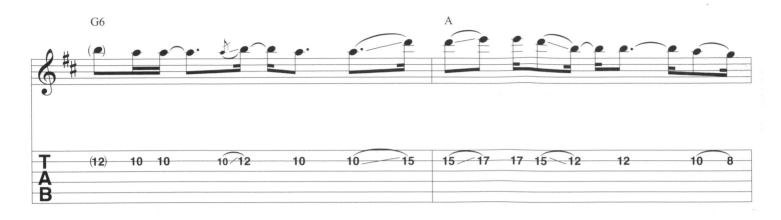

Interlude

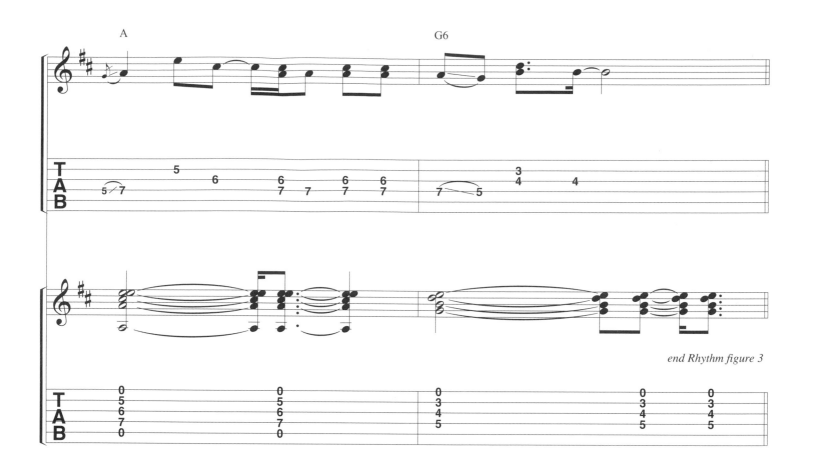

Bass solo

acoustic guitar with Rhythm figure 3

D.S. al Coda

play eight times

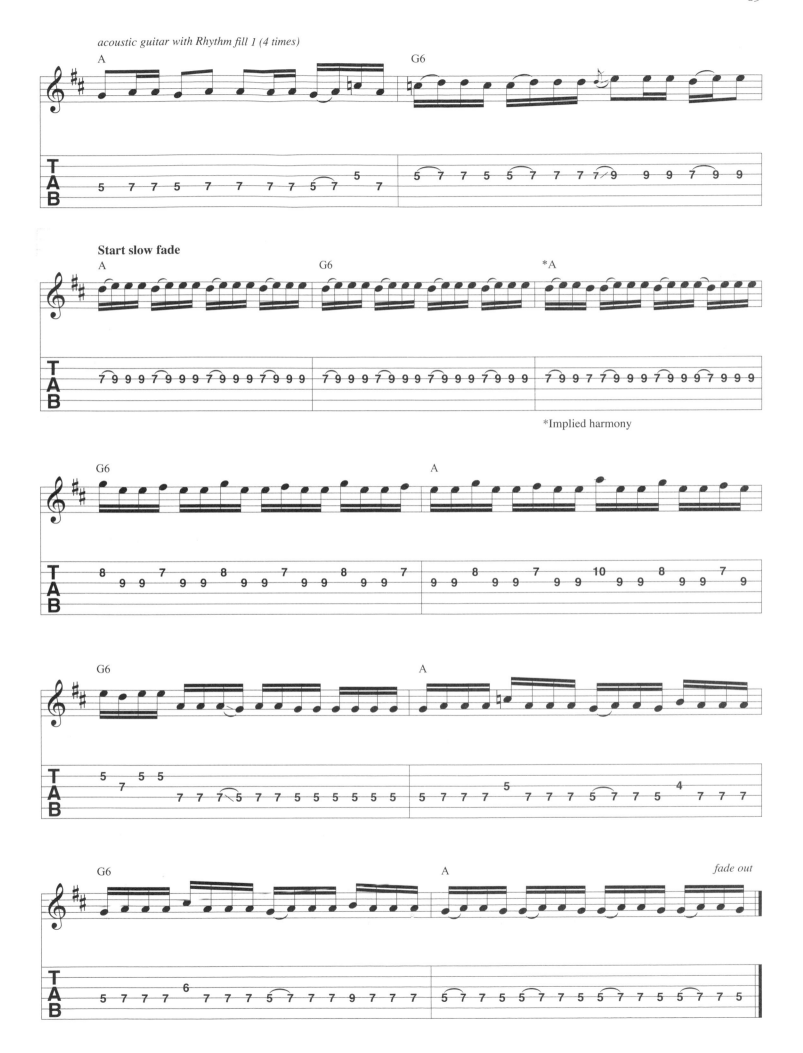

driving song

By John F. Bell, Michael N. Houser, Todd A. Nance and David Schools

violin with ad lib on D.C.

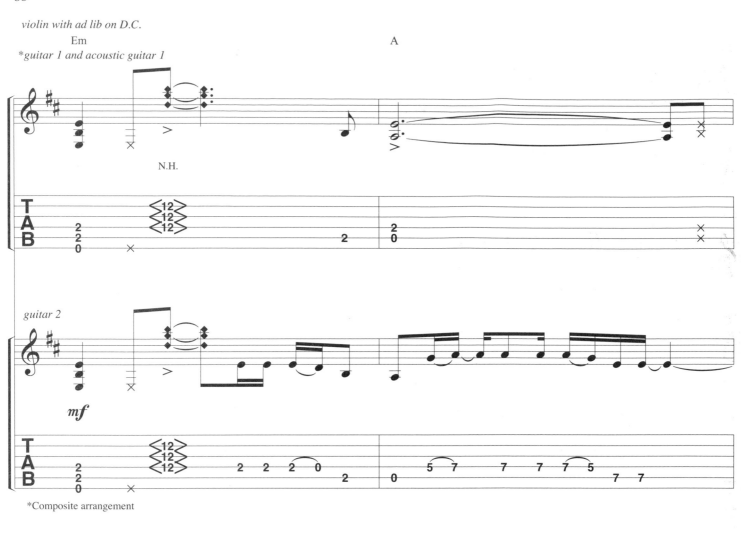

*Composite arrangement

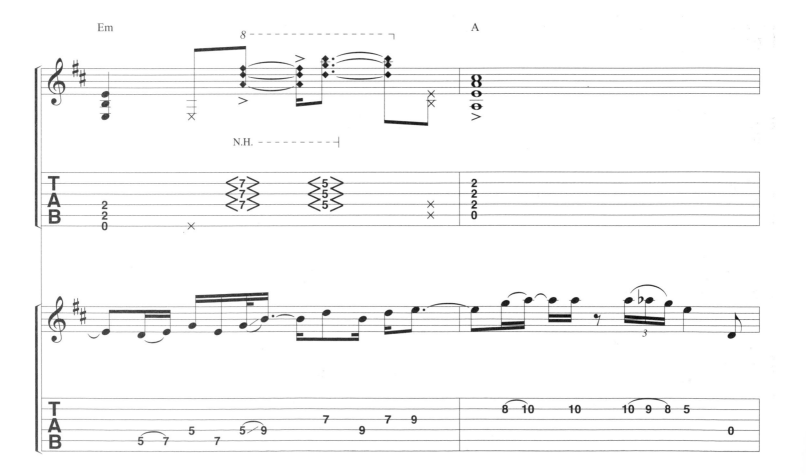

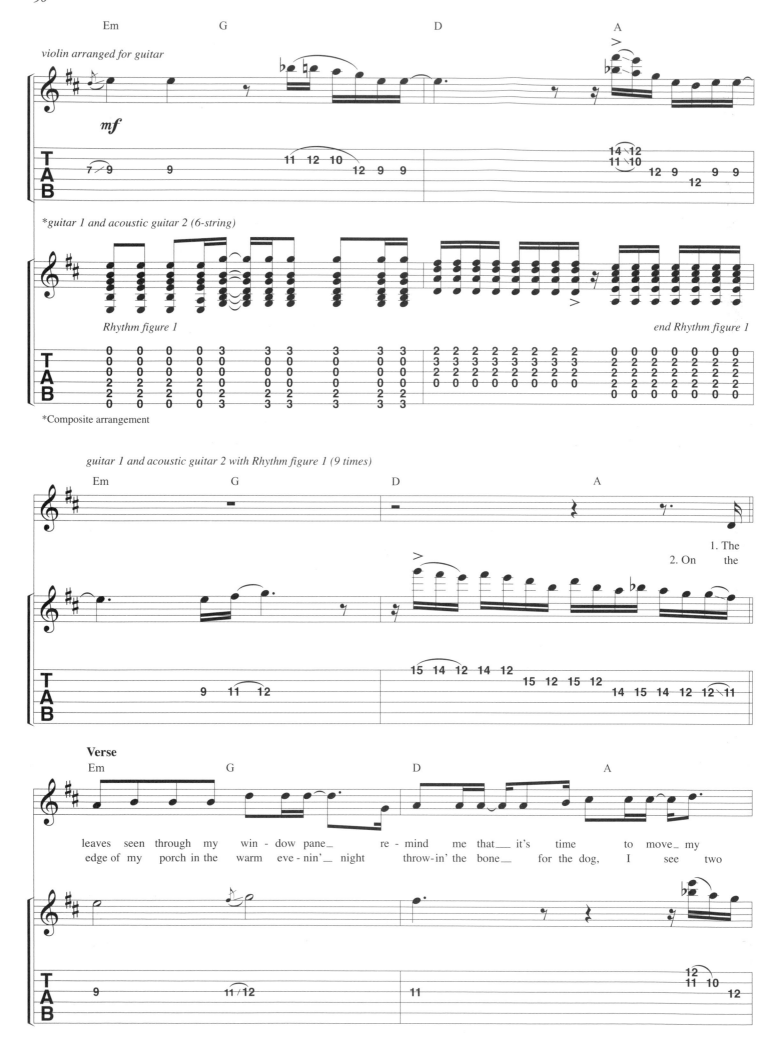

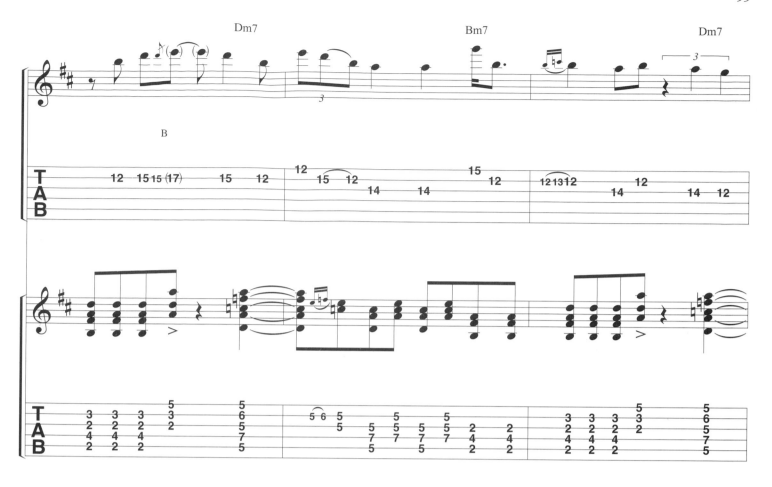

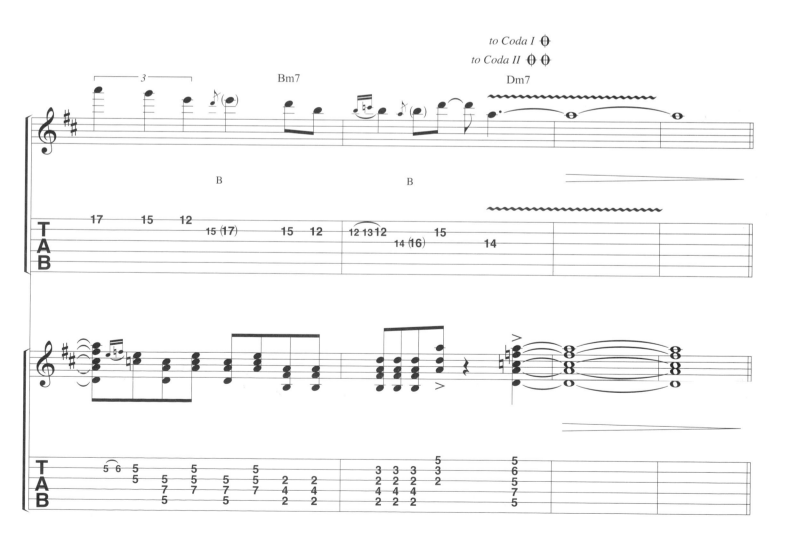

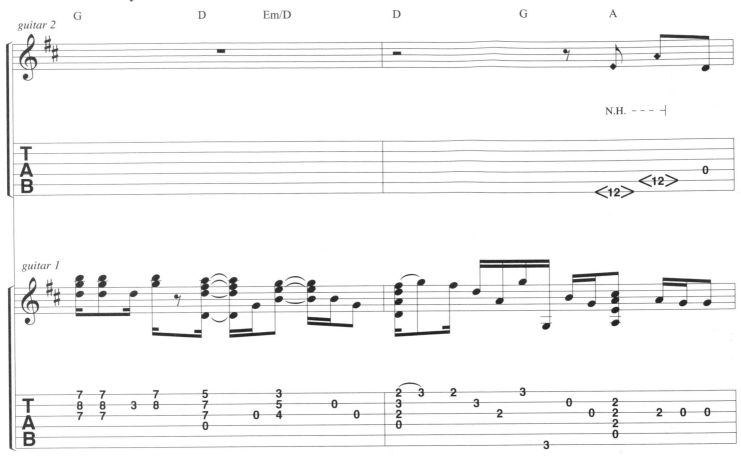

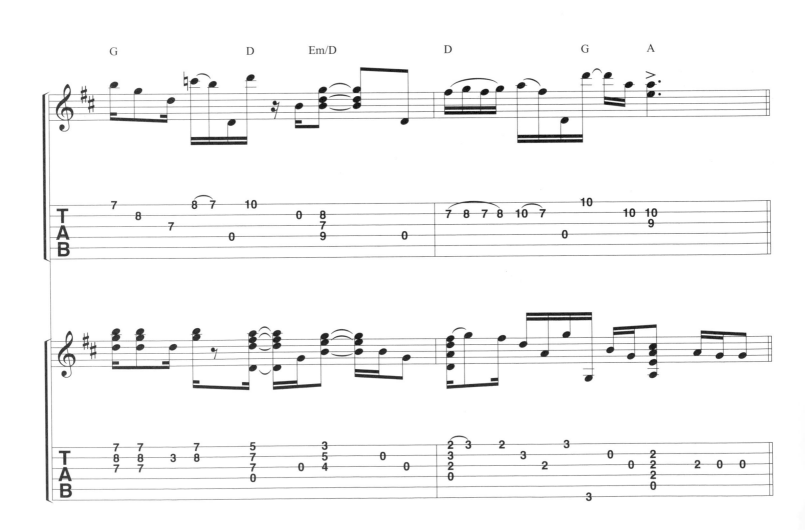

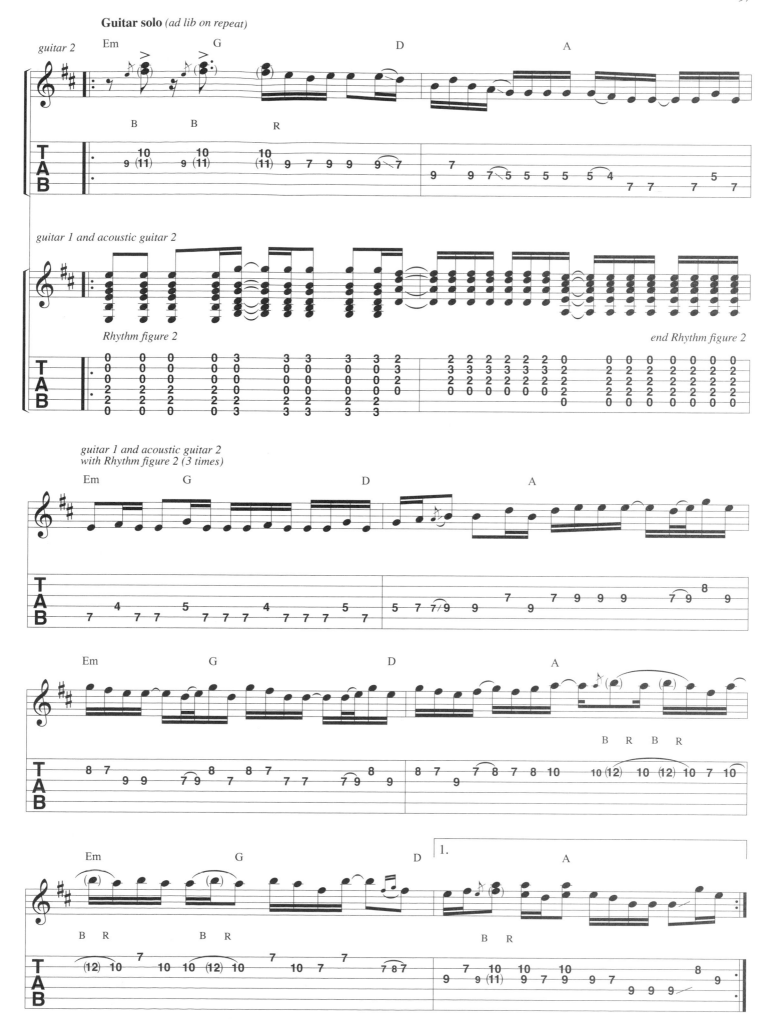

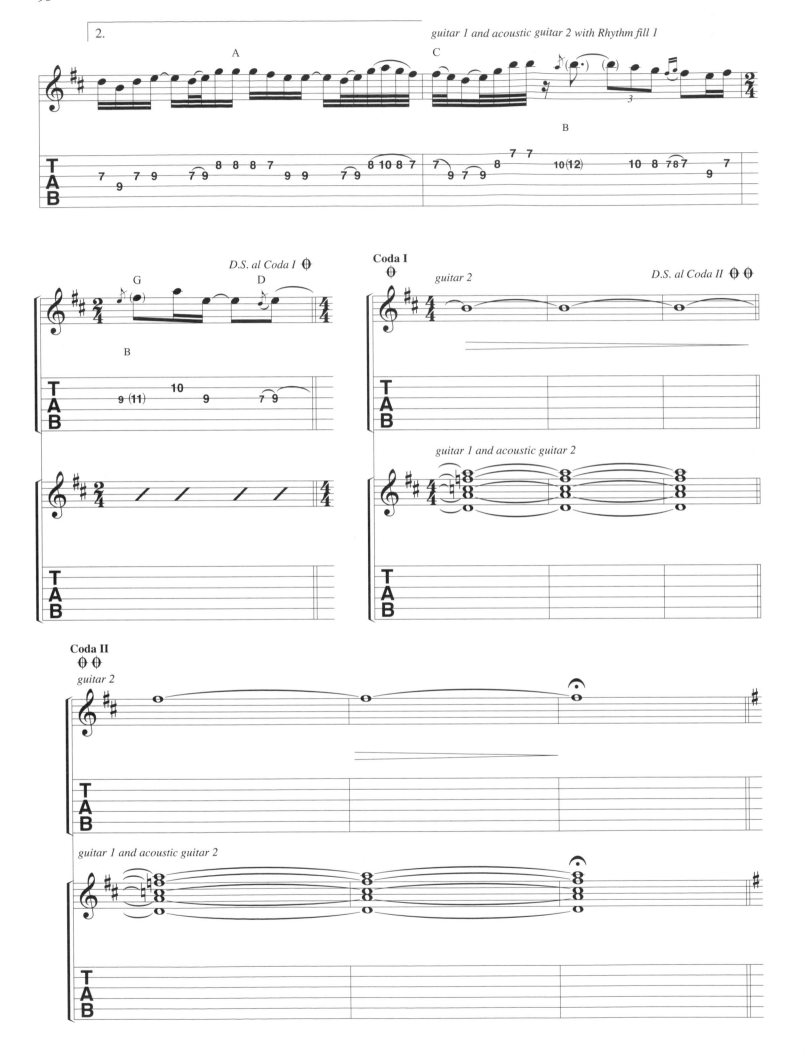

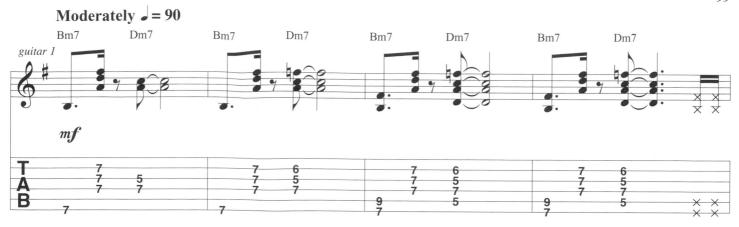

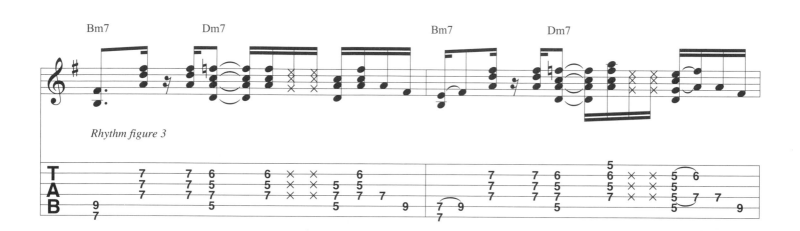

holden oversoul

By John F. Bell, Michael N. Houser, Todd A. Nance and David Schools

Verse

guitar 1 and acoustic guitar with Rhythm figure 1 (2 times)

screen door to the farm - er's porch,_____ to the back porch,_____
last of Nov - em - ber passed_____ with his new life,_____

3. See additional lyrics

_____ to the back land._____ Well, it's
_____ with his new wife, said she was

nev - er left_____ closed._____ Ah, the
fel - ing a - lit - tle cold. But then the

new air pushed a full_____ wind that brought_____ worlds on through_
ghost of a clown just danced in and did a few tricks

that on - ly he could_ know.
and danced out a - gain. Warm - ing a farm - er's_ soul._

1. _____ **2.**

_____ 2. And as the

guitar 2 (with clean tone)

mp

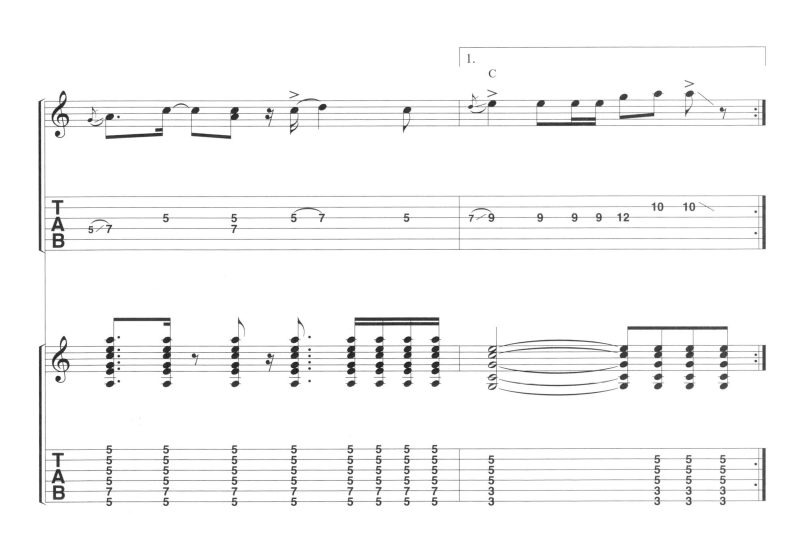

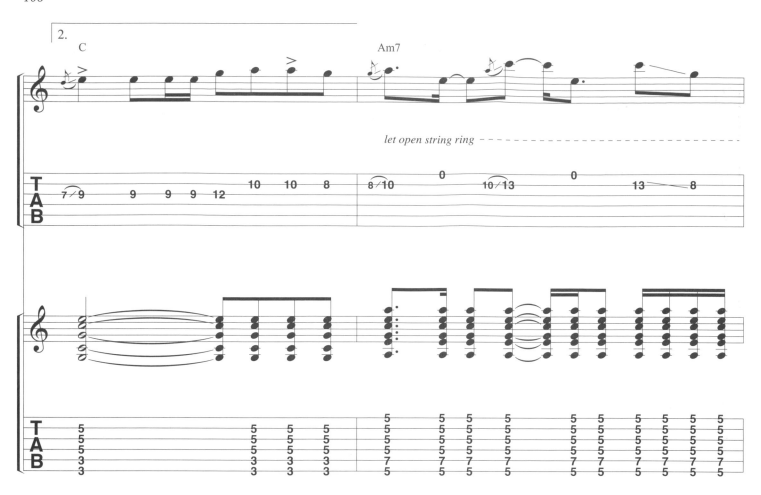

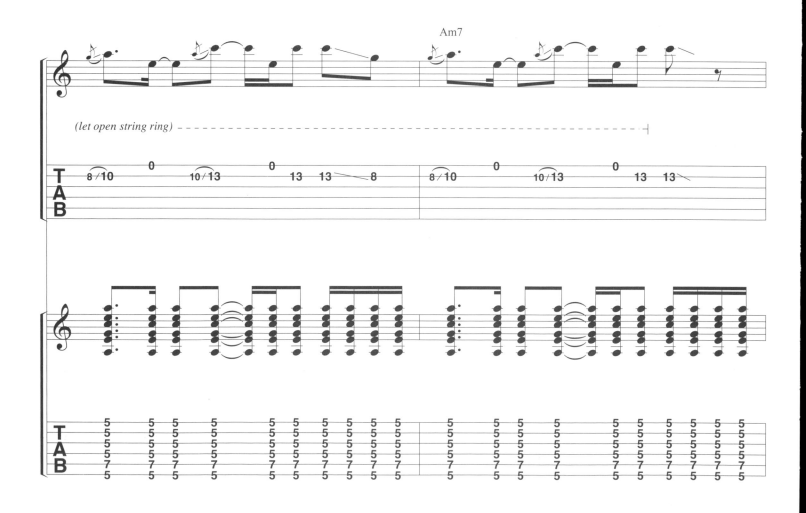

Moderately, in 2 ♩ = 144

D.S. al Coda

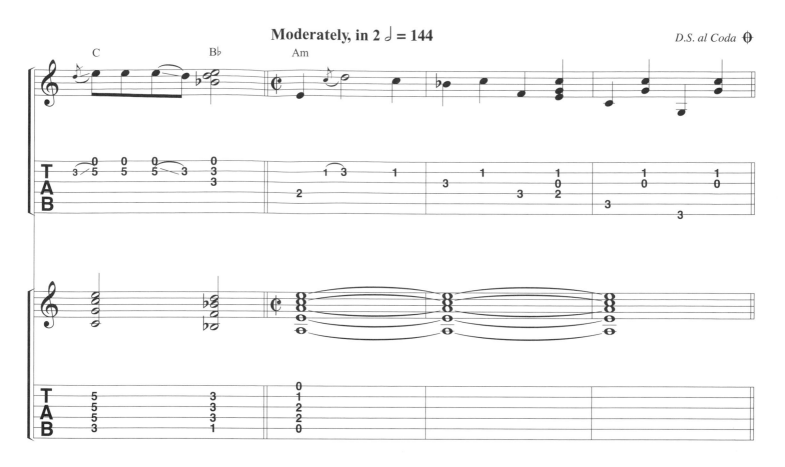

Coda

Moderately ♩ = 144

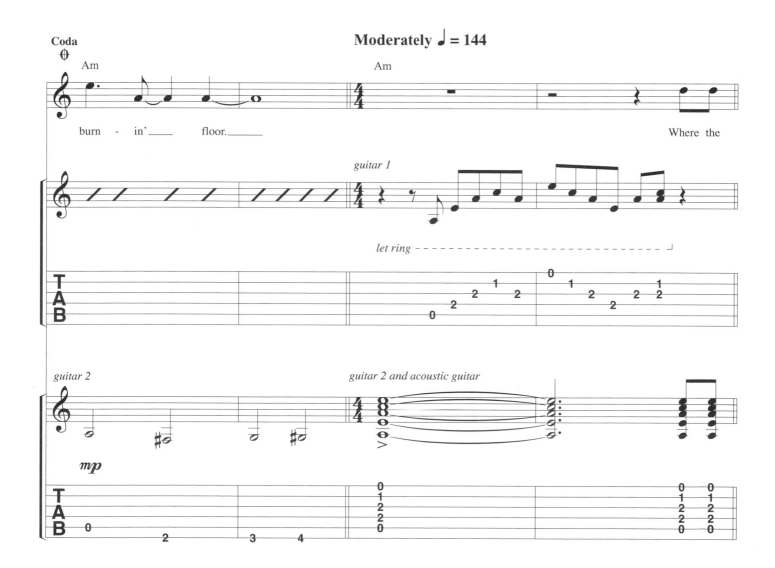

burn - in' ____ floor. ____

Where the

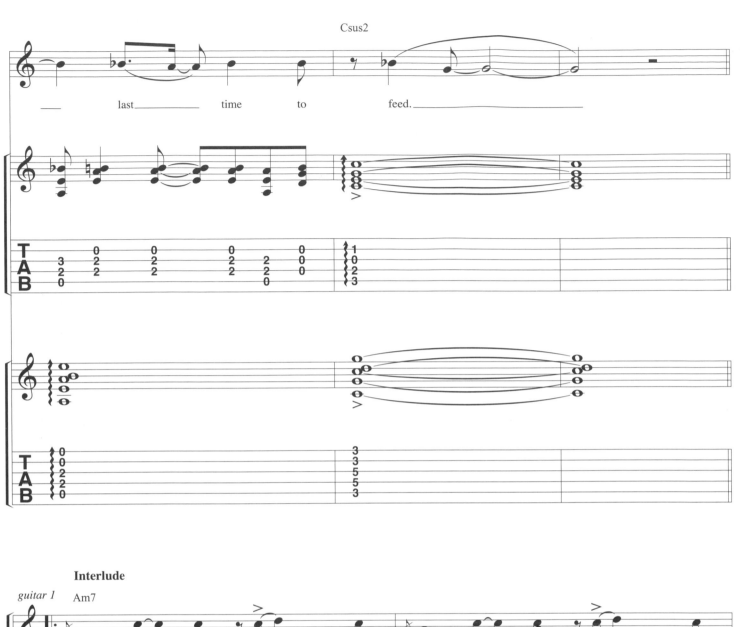

last____ time to feed._____

Interlude

guitar 1 Am7

guitar 2 and acoustic guitar

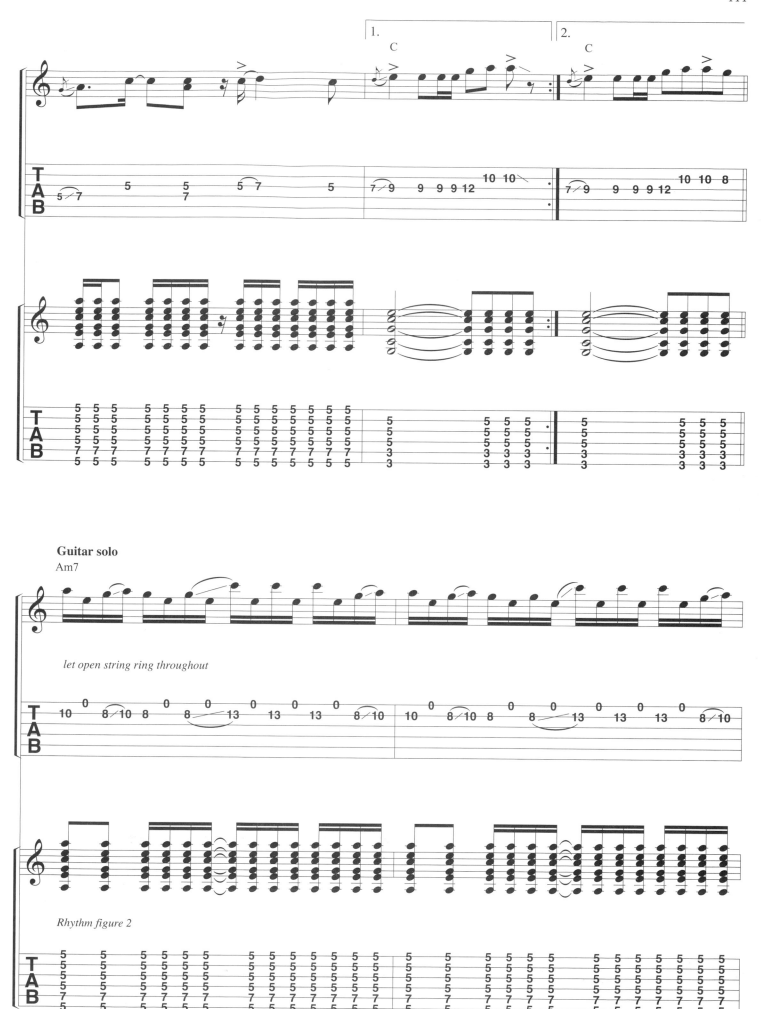

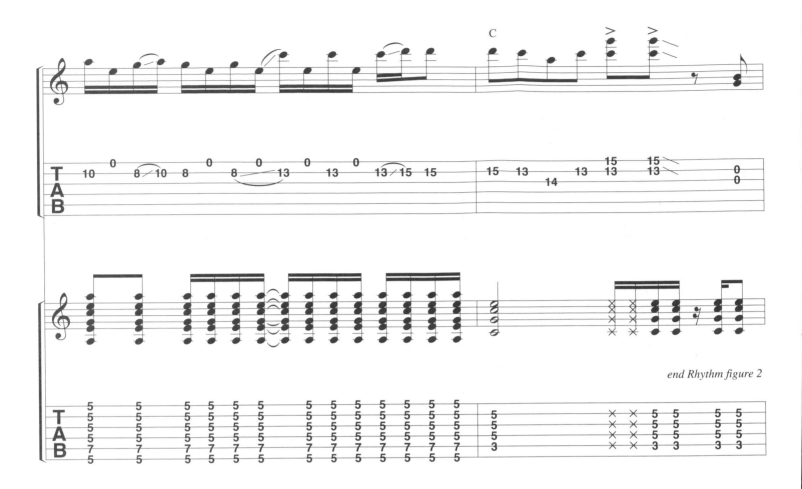

end Rhythm figure 2

guitar 2 and acoustic guitar with Rhythm figure 2

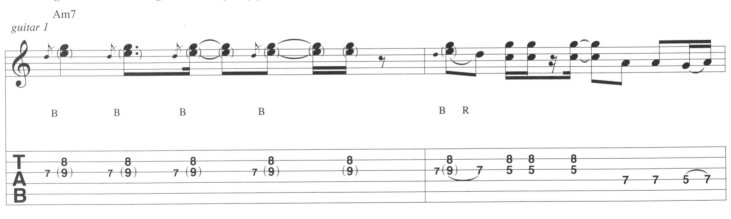

let open string ring throughout

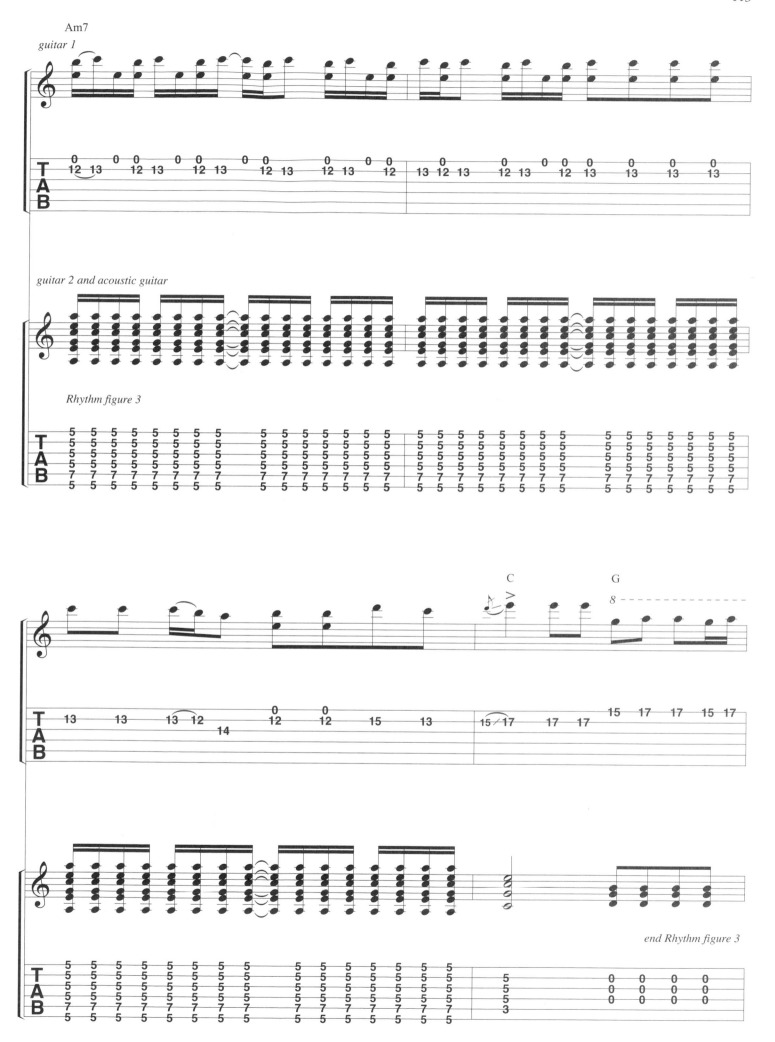

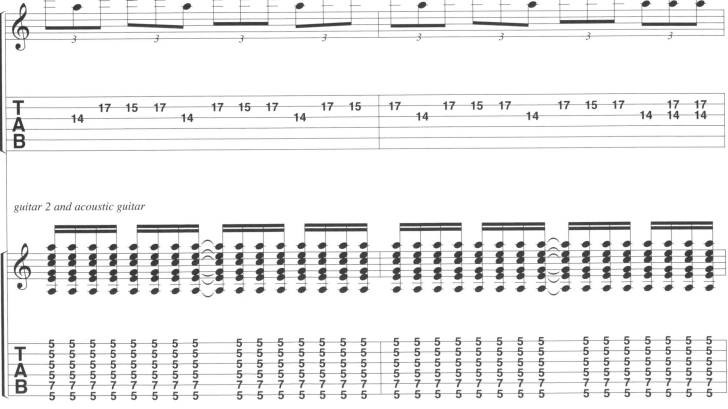

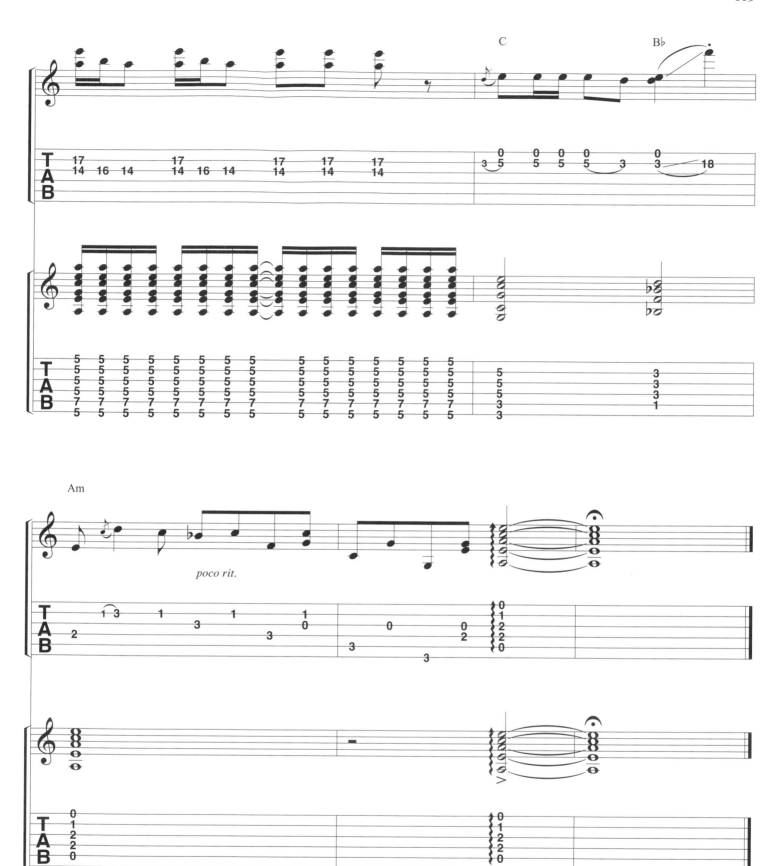

Verse

3. Summer was all there was.
We were working, breathing heat.
Terror rising out of control.
Through that door came a breeze,
Wrapped on through our heads
And around our spines,
Cooling off the burning floor.

contentment blues

By John F. Bell, Michael N. Houser, Todd A. Nance and David Schools

Slowly ♩. = **66**

Freely

Verses 1 and 3

guitars 1 and 2 with Rhythm figure 1 (3 1/2 times)

hard - lipped   wom - an   nag - ging   at   who   I   should   be.   The

blue   lights   round - ing   the   cor - ner,   they're   not   turn - in'   for   no   one   like

guitar 1 with Rhythm fill 1   *guitars 1 and 2 with Rhythm figure 1 (4 times)*

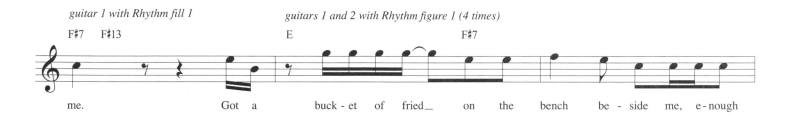

me.   Got   a   buck - et   of   fried__   on   the   bench   be - side   me,   e - nough

chick - en   for   one   man's___   needs.   Life's   been   get - tin'   a   lit - tle   bit   eas -

to Coda

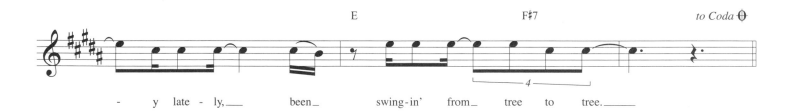

- y   late - ly,___   been__   swing - in'   from__   tree   to   tree._____

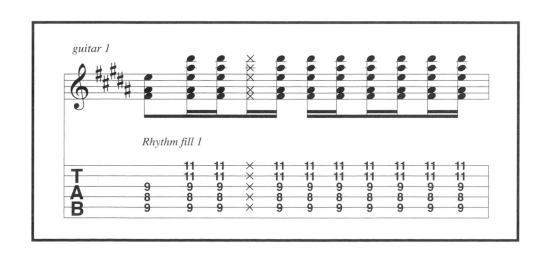

Chorus
guitars 1 and 2 with Rhythm figure 1 (4 times)

I love my chick - en, I love my chick - en in the tree.

— 2. There's some

Verse 2
guitars 1 and 2 with Rhythm figure 1 (12 times)

— good moves of a life - time, mov - in' on back to fav - or

these times. And to work - in', mov - ing it

to see. All those good things I've done com - in' on

back to take care of me, take care of, to take care of me.

You don't need to pay a dol - lar for your dues if all you're

plan - nin' on play - in' are Con - tent - ment Blues.

Interlude

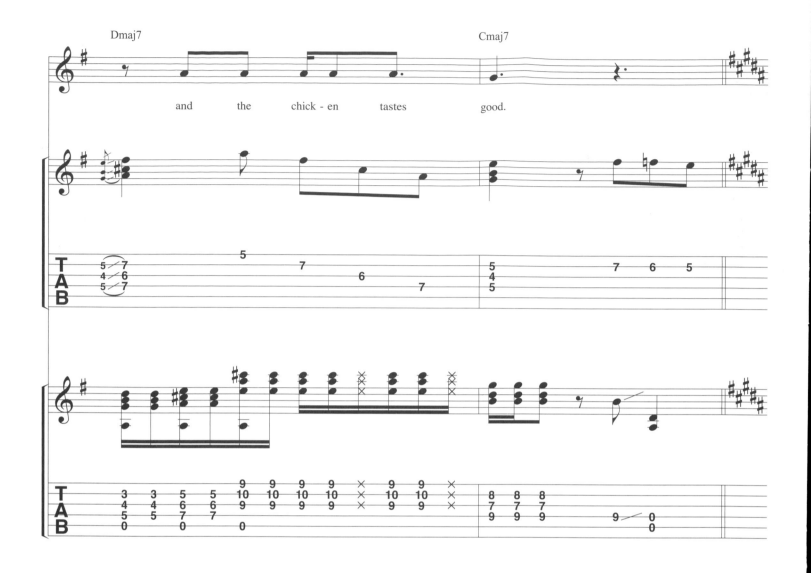

Chorus

guitars 1 and 2 with Rhythm figure 1 (4 times)

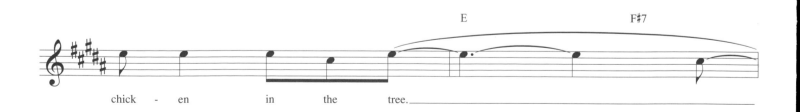

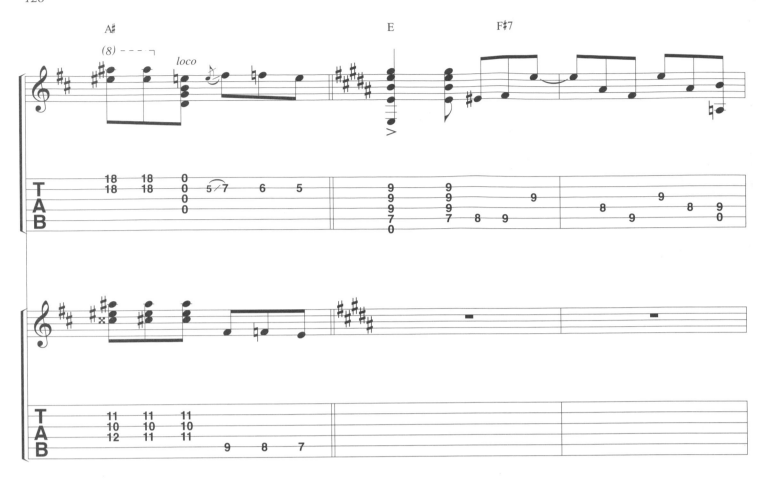